20

Truths

To Grow Your Faith

Debbie Stuart

20 Truths to Grow Your Faith

Breakthrough Christian Publishing

www.breakthroughchristianpublishing.com

©2025 by Debbie Stuart

Unless otherwise noted, Scripture quotations are taken from the Holy Bible, New International Version®, NIV®. Copyright © 1973, 1978, 1984, 2011 by Biblica, Inc.™ Used by permission of Zondervan.

Scripture quotations marked (MSG) or The Message are taken from The Message Bible. Copyright 1993, 1994, 1995, 1996, 2000, 2001, 2002. Used by permission of NavPress Publishing Group.

Scripture quotations marked (NLT) are taken from the Holy Bible, New Living Translation, copyright © 1996, 2004, 2007 by Tyndale House Foundation. Used by permission of Tyndale House Publishers, Inc., Carol Stream, Illinois 60188. All rights reserved.

Scripture quotations marked (NASB) are taken from the Holy Bible: New American Standard Bible. Copyright © 1995, 2020. LaHabra, CA: The Lockman Foundation. Used by permission. All rights reserved.

Scripture quotations marked (ESV) are taken from The Holy Bible, English Standard Version ® (ESV®), copyright © 2001 by Crossway, a publishing ministry of Good News Publishers. Used by permission.

Scripture quotations marked (NKJV) are taken from the New King James Version®. Copyright © 1982 by Thomas Nelson. Used by permission. All rights reserved.

Scripture quotations marked (CSB) are taken from the Christian Standard Bible®, Copyright © 2017 by Holman Bible Publishers. Used by permission. Christian Standard Bible® and CSB® are federally registered trademarks of Holman Bible Publishers.

Scripture quotations marked (KJV) are taken from the KING JAMES VERSION (KJV), which is in the public domain.

Scripture quotations marked (AMP) are taken from the Amplified® Bible, Copyright © 1954, 1958, 1962, 1964, 1965, 1987 by the Lockman Foundation. Used by permission.

Scripture quotations marked (AMPC) are taken from The Classic Edition, Amplified Bible, Copyright © 1987 by the Lockman Foundation. Used by permission. All rights reserved.

Published 2025

Printed in the United States of America

30 29 28 27 26 25   1 2 3 4 5

ISBN: 979-8-9935753-0-8 paperback
ISBN: 979-8-9935753-1-5 eBook
Library of Congress: 1-15055461591

Dedication

This book is dedicated to women ... everywhere, in every generation.

*My call to women's ministry came through the loss of one great woman—
my mom, Carol Self.*

*My love for it came through the many women
the Lord has brought across my path.*

A heartfelt thank you to those who have prayed for me through these years.

And to my mother-in-law, Shirley Stuart, whose faith is now sight.

*May we forever speak truth into one another's lives
and champion each other's faith!*

*"So, go now and write all this down. Put it in a book so that the record will be
there to instruct the coming generations ..." (Isa. 30:8 MSG).*

*"This is what the LORD, the God of Israel, says: 'Write in a book all the words
that I have spoken to you'" (Jer. 30:2).*

I pray the Lord will be glorified through these words.

Contents

Introduction

What you hold in your hand is a labor of love and an act of obedience. It is my meager attempt to put on paper what the Lord has taught me and walked me through. It is my prayer that it will be beneficial to you and help you grow in your walk with the Lord.

What you feed grows.

Growth doesn't happen by accident. Faith is more than belief—it's a living journey that deepens with every step we take. It grows in moments of peace and is tested in seasons of doubt. Like a seed planted in fertile soil, faith needs care, nourishment, and time to mature into something strong and unshakable.

This book is an invitation to grow—to strengthen your walk with the Lord, to see His hand in the everyday, and to walk confidently even when the path is uncertain. Through Scripture, Biblical principles, and practical application, we'll explore how faith can move from something we talk about to something we walk out every day.

No matter where you are in your spiritual walk, this journey will remind you that faith isn't about perfection—it's about progress, persistence, and a heart that keeps turning toward God. Let's start with 20 Minutes a Day

May your faith grow deeper with every page!

Debbie Stuart

Chapter One

Grit Don't Quit

"Therefore … sisters, stand firm. Let nothing move you. Always give yourselves fully to the work of the Lord, because you know that your labor in the Lord is not in vain."
1 Corinthians 15:58

NITTY GRITTY

Born and raised in Louisiana, I am a Southern girl (which explains things as you keep reading). We have unusual phrases and use different words to describe the point we want to make. One phrase: "THE NITTY GRITTY!"

The nitty gritty is the most important aspect or details of a subject or situation. And that's what I'd like to share with you, hoping it will encourage "your socks off." So, open your Bible to 1 Corinthians 15:58. This is our **focus verse** for this lesson. Something that is helpful for future reference is to highlight this in your Bible.

"Therefore … sisters, stand firm. Let nothing move you. Always give yourselves fully to the work of the Lord, because you know that your labor in the Lord is not in vain" (1 Cor. 15:58).

Another translation says, "So … sisters, be **strong** and **immovable.** Always work enthusiastically for the Lord, for you know that nothing you do for the Lord is ever useless" (NLT, emphasis mine).

The ESV version says, "Therefore … be **steadfast**, immovable, always abounding in the work of the Lord, knowing that in the Lord your labor is not in vain" (emphasis mine).

From this verse, the word *steadfast* is defined as "fixed with a purpose." Another Southern word I love is GRIT! You will often here me say, "Grit don't quit!" And I strive to be *gritty*. *Steadfast* describes what it means to have GRIT. Psychologists and researchers have indicated that grit enables a person to succeed more than skill, IQ, and talent.

Grit is defined as:

- Courage, resolve, strength of character
- Perseverance and passion for achieving long-term goals without quitting
- Tenacity (determination) to do hard things
- Working with determination toward a challenge and maintaining a constant effort despite setbacks and moments of failure

Gritty women make progress, not excuses. **Grit don't quit!**

In Angela Duckworth's book *Grit: The Power of Passion and Perseverance*, she indicates that grit is not a talent or skill, **but a decision**! She takes a psychological and neuroscientific approach about how grit starts in the mind and how moods and emotions often leave us gritless. Now, let's unpack these definitions using Scripture, especially the last definition.

STAND FIRM

What does it mean to be strong, steadfast, and immovable, especially through difficulties, hardships, and setbacks?

As I studied in the book of Ezra, I was shocked to see what felt looked like my life playing out on the pages of God's Word. There are so many life lessons in this book of the Bible! Let's look at a few for a better understanding of how we can be strong, steadfast, and immovable.

In the first chapter of the book of Ezra, we read that God **prompted and motivated Ezra.** God was working in him and, as a believer, God is working in you! The Lord gave Ezra an assignment. Ladies, you are reading this on assignment from God. You aren't reading this by accident! One commentator said that Ezra not only had a relationship with God, but he also had a relationship with God's Word!

How do we have a relationship with God's Word? The way to have this relationship is this: Spend time with

> # God's plans, direction, and activities are closely related to His Word.

Him. It really is that simple. Just like you get to know someone by spending time with them, you will get to know God by spending time with Him. I like to say it like this: "Twenty Minutes a Day for the Rest of Your Life." That means twenty minutes of reading, studying, and praying God's Word each day. It will change your life. God's plans, direction, and activities are closely related to His Word. Develop a relationship with it, and your relationship with God will be strengthened.

COMPLETE DEVOTION

Ezra 4:4–5 reveals that the enemy tried to *frighten, isolate, discourage, intimidate, and frustrate the aim of the children of Israel!* These are enemy tactics that we need to be aware of. Ezra was aware. He did not have a casual commitment with the Lord. His devotion was complete. The apostle Paul was also fully devoted and committed. Acts 20:24 reveals his response to the hardship he endured: "My only aim is to finish the race and complete the task the Lord Jesus has given me."

The following verses give us spiritual strategies against enemy tactics. Here's how to fight enemy opposition:

- Ezra 7:10 – He set his mind to study God's Word, to do God's Word, and to teach God's Word. To do God's Word means to practice, to obey, to live, and just DO IT! The Bible says in James 1:22 not to be hearers only of God's Word, but to be doers. Psalm 119:34 (NLT) says, "Give me understanding and I will obey your instructions; I will put them into practice with all my heart."

- Ezra 7:28 – "Because the hand of the LORD my God was on me, I took courage." This reminds us that God is *with* us, and He is *working in* us. He gives us courage and makes us brave.
- Ezra 10:4 (ESV) – "Arise, for it is your task, and we are with you; be strong and do it." Darlin' (another Southern term), it's time for you to rise up! Rise up out of ashes; get up out of chaos and confusion. Move forward in faith and stop circling in the wilderness. Grit don't quit!

This is how Paul puts it in Galatians 1:3–4, from *The Message* Bible:

> *You crazy Galatians! Did someone put a spell on you? Have you taken leave of your senses? Something crazy has happened, for it's obvious that you no longer have the crucified Jesus in clear focus in your lives. His sacrifice on the cross was certainly set before you clearly enough. Let me put this question to you: How did your new life begin? Was it by working your heads off to please God? Or was it by responding to God's Message to you? Are you going to continue this craziness? For only crazy people would think they could complete by their own efforts what was begun by God. If you weren't smart enough or strong enough to begin it, how do you suppose you could perfect it? Did you go through this whole painful learning process for nothing? It is not yet a total loss, but it certainly will be if you keep this up!*

Let's look at habits and behaviors that will enable us to rise up even in the midst of difficulties. In my life (I am sixty as I write this), there have been two main areas that cause me trouble. Two categories where I seem to get stuck and off track in my walk with the Lord. The first is fear. The second is feelings. Fear paralyzes and feelings create excuses.

In Exodus 6:9, the Bible tells us this about the Israelites. They didn't follow God because they had a broken spirit and hard labor. Hard labor means God gave them a hard assignment. They were paralyzed by fear and created excuses. Excuses cause us to quit. But **grit don't quit**! Feelings create all the other craziness in our life with emotions that drive us to a dark place, attitudes that talk us out of the will of

God, and negative words that are destructive. Time with the Lord (Twenty Minutes a Day for the Rest of Your Life) increases faith, and faith ignites perseverance for changed lives!

Looking back at Ezra in chapter 1, God prompted King Cyrus to do something. To prompt is to cause or bring about action or feeling—encouraging someone who is hesitant. God moved in the heart of Ezra and roused his sprit.

What assignment has God given you?

What is God prompting you to do? Is God stirring and motivating you toward a specific action? Is God asking you to start doing something new? Or maybe He's asking you to stop doing something? What assignment has God given you?

Or have you been hesitant in some area of your life? Are you hesitant about confessing sin, forgiving someone, being completely devoted to Christ, serving in some area, or committing to daily Bible study? If so, I have great news for you: "For God is working in you, giving you the desire and the power to do what pleases him" (Phil. 2:13 NLT). What else do you need but God's power to do what He asks of us? We are all without excuse. To help keep believing this I set a reminder in my phone to send me a notification at 2:13 every day to remind me that God gives me desire and power to do what pleases Him.

But guess what happened to Ezra immediately following the prompting of the Lord? It was the intimidation of the enemy.

- The Lord gave Ezra an assignment.
- And then, the enemy gave him opposition.

One tactic of the enemy is intimidation. This we learn from Ezra's story. Let me jerk the cover off of this tactic: It means to frighten or cause worry, stress, or anxiety. He's been successful at doing this in my own life. Has he been successful in yours?

It may sound something like this:

- "Now what are you going to do? God doesn't care about you. What if *this* happens or what if *this* doesn't happen?"
- "This is such a waste of time. Nothing is going to change. Nothing good is coming from this. It is the worst possible outcome, and you'll never get over it."
- "Nobody likes you. You don't have any friends. You'll never get married. You'll never have children. God was cruel to take your spouse, your mother, your child, your health."

Sound familiar? Intrusive thoughts and negative narratives cycle endlessly through our minds until we believe it. The enemy's tactic according to Ezra 4:1–4 is to *infiltrate, disrupt, counterfeit, discourage, and frustrate your aim.* What is your aim? From Paul, we learn it is to finish the assignment given by God.

Let's do a quick and honest self-evaluation: Has the enemy been at work in your life and mind? Has he been successful with his attempts to intimidate, disrupt, discourage, and frustrate? I thought so! It's as old as Adam and Eve. In the story of Adam and Eve in Genesis, the enemy lied to them and created doubt. They disobeyed the Lord, sinned, and then hid. God came after them, pursuing them (just like He is pursuing YOU!). God asked them, "Why are you hiding?" They said, "We are naked." And the Lord said, "Who told you that you were naked?" (Gen. 3:11).

WHO TOLD YOU THAT?

"I can't get over what happened." Who told you that? Read Philippians 3:13–14.

"Well, I can't help how I feel." Who told you that? Isaiah 26:3 (ESV) tells us, "You keep him in perfect peace whose mind is stayed on you."

"I can't do this anymore!" Who told you that? You can do all things through Christ who gives you strength! In 2 Timothy 1:7, it says, "For the Spirit God gave us does not make us timid, but gives us power, love and self-discipline."

God wired us and made us to be strong and steadfast, to fight and to win. I know from experience how His strength helps us out of the pit when life is hard. I know what it's like to have hard assignments. I lost my mom to a devastating battle with cancer when she was forty. I was twenty-three and had a five-week-old baby boy. I buried my dad at an early age due to alcoholism. I buried my father-in-law and all my grandparents. I lost two nephews due to their addictions. My husband had a heart transplant in 2020. My daughter lived 2,200 miles away for nine years, and my son spent ten years in prison due to drug addiction. After all of that, I buried a baby granddaughter, Abigail Jean, when she was born. I know what it's like to have a hard assignment.

This is what I used to think. Nobody knows what I am going through! Nobody knows how I feel! And nobody cares! They didn't know because I didn't tell them. I hid my pain in the same way Eve hid her sin. Nobody knows and nobody cares. Who told you that???

Don't wimp out, don't whine, and don't quit seeking Jesus!

But God gives us what it takes to be strong and courageous. We are to stand on His Word as our foundation and life. This Word is Jesus who became flesh and dwelt among us. He is still with us today by His Spirit. And we can be transformed by the renewing of our minds according to Romans 12:1–2. Look up these verses and give thanks to God for renewing our minds with His Word.

We need one another in those hard times. God tells us two are better than one, for they can help each other succeed. When one falls down, the other can pick them up (see Ecclesiastes 4:10).

Matthew chapter 9 tells the story of a woman with an issue (raise your hand right now if you have an issue). She said to herself, "If I can get to Jesus, I will be healed." And she did, and she was! Jesus said to her, "Take heart, daughter … your faith has healed you" (Matt. 9:22). And from that very moment she was healed. **Who told her that? The Lord Jesus told her that!** The enemy had been telling her for years that there was nothing she could do about this, that she would never be healed, but Jesus …

She didn't wimp out, whine, or wear out. She just kept seeking Jesus. Hers is an example to follow: Don't wimp out, don't whine, and don't quit seeking Jesus! We give too much mental real estate to problems, pressures, and irritations about things we cannot control. Before you know it, you are living a frustrating life when what we want to live is a resilient life, where GRIT DON'T QUIT!

THE BEAUTY OF IRRITATION

A pearl is made by a little piece of grit. It gets into the tissue of the oyster. Then through the irritating process, it makes a beautiful pearl. God may have allowed something irritating in your life because He is in the process of creating you to be a beautiful pearl of great value. Think of the significance of knowing Proverbs 31:25: "She is clothed with strength and dignity; she can laugh at the days to come." How could she be and do these things? There was probably grit in her life. Irritation used by God to give strength and joy.

Don't give the enemy a stick to beat you with! Don't let him into your headspace. Pay attention to what you say to yourself: "That's just the way I am …" We may think that in the moment, but we can all be transformed, changed by the Word of God and a relationship with Him.

"I can't work Bible study time into my schedule. I don't understand Scripture." Who told you that? Think about it. If God gives strength, dignity, and joy, where then does weakness, shame, and unhappiness come from? It is not from God.

Second Corinthians 10:4–5 tells us to bring all our thoughts captive under obedience to Christ. Your thoughts don't get to run rough-shod all over your mind! "We demolish arguments and every pretension that sets itself up against the knowledge of God, and we take captive every thought to make it obedient to Christ" (2 Cor. 10:4–5).

Negative thoughts and actions are destructive to our faith and emotions. Let me give you a personal example. This week someone said something I didn't agree with. I knew they didn't know the whole story. Immediately, I felt the Lord impress upon me to let it go, not to get into this, and not to say a word. My mind said, "Yes, Sir. I will just let this go and not say a word."

BUT MY MOUTH apparently did not get the message. My mouth would not let it go! Our minds and our mouths can get us into trouble!!! Go ahead and add that to the two categories next to fear and feelings. Being aware of how easily the enemy can get us off track in our thinking and recognizing this tactic will go a long way in keeping us out of trouble and keeping us strong and resilient

Focus Verse

"Therefore … sisters, stand firm. Let nothing move you. Always give yourselves fully to the work of the Lord, because you know that your labor in the Lord is not in vain"
(1 Cor. 15:58).

Our focus verse from 1 Corinthians 15:58 tells us to stand firm. What does it mean to stand firm? Google this question and write what you discover.

_____

_____

_____

_____

_____

_____

_____

What does it mean to give fully to God's work? Look this up and write your answer. Read Philippians 4:8 for insight.

_____

_____

_____

_____

Connecting the Dots

How does our focus verse fit with what you read about Ezra?

_____

_____

_____

_____

_____

Make It Personal

How does this apply to your faith and ability to stand firm when your assignment is hard?

_____

_____

_____

_____

Do you have a personal relationship with God? If you are unsure, read how you can have this relationship on page 209.

Do you have a relationship with God's Word? What did you learn from this lesson for how you can do so?

_____

_____

_____

_____

SUMMARY

I know there is a new trend or maybe a counseling tool that tells us that we need to feel all our feelings—ALL the FEELS! I understand the idea behind not pushing your feelings down. I get that! But, careful, let's not swing what was intended to be *helpful* to something that is *harmful.* You don't need to get all in your feelings! Raise your hand if in the last ten days you got all into your feelings about something. The truth is there are some feelings we don't need to live with. Instead, we need to repent them! *No, she did not just say that!* I did!

Feelings of resentment, jealousy, shame, guilt, anger, hurt, comparison, and pride—we don't need to feel all that. They don't need to be rehashed. They need to be confessed. When the enemy tells you that you are broken, asks what's wrong with you, says you can't do this … at that moment, ask yourself, "Who told me that?" We should not tell ourselves, "I am so tired, overwhelmed, anxious, stressed, and worried." We should tell ourselves, "If I can just get to Jesus, I will be just fine."

God tells us we are overcomers, and we have divine strength. His death on the cross redeems us, and the Holy Spirit lives in us! He is at work and grit don't quit

Begin today by implementing new habits and new thought processes. Just as Ezra had an assignment from God, we do too:

- Stand firm.
- Be fully devoted.

- Do the hard labor.
- Hold every thought captive in obedience to Christ.
- Think on those things of excellence.

Start Twenty Minutes a Day for the Rest of Your Life in God's Word and a relationship with Him. Live your life in such a way that you make the devil sorry he messed with you in the first place. And that, darlin', is the *nitty gritty*!

Grit don't quit and your labor is not in vain.

Note: This complete message can be viewed at www.greenacreswomen.org under the Teaching tab, or search the title: "Nitty Gritty."

Chapter Two

Cultivate Joy

"Dear ... sisters, when troubles of any kind come your way,
consider it an opportunity for great joy.
For you know that when your faith is tested,
your endurance has a chance to grow. So let it grow,
for when your endurance is fully developed,
you will be perfect and complete, needing nothing."
James 1:2–4 (NLT)

Often when trouble comes my way, it is an opportunity for me to whine and complain, beg and plead, fuss and fume. Then I may develop a nice "Southern attitude" to go with it. But God's Word says He allows trouble to come our way so we can develop endurance and perseverance. I will explain more about that in a later paragraph.

For several months, the Lord has been teaching me one thing over and over! I cannot tell you how many life experiences have lined up around this one thing. I am confident the lesson is not just for me or only about me and am hopeful it will benefit you as well.

That one thing I have been taught is this: How to carry sorrow and celebration at the same time. How to cultivate joy while also working through great challenges. How to consider it joy when your faith is tested, when your heart is broken, and your dreams have been shattered.

It all started in December. I was laughing and enjoying grandkids during the day. I was excited and happy about some things we had been praying for. My youngest grandson, Gunner, was about three years old. I guess he perceived something was going on with Dodie (my grandmother name). He put both elbows on the table and clasped his little hands under his chin and said, "Dodie, I happy!" and I smiled so big. Then he said, "Dodie, you happy?" And it was all I could do to hold back the hot tears that flooded my eyes. It was hard to control the wave of emotions.

I was happy. Spending time with grandkids makes me very happy. But *at the same time* I was heartbroken, because we were working through a dark time which grieved me terribly. Daytime was lots of fun with grandkids, but at night when things got quiet, I cried into my pillow. I thought to myself, "I am fourteen shades of crazy here! I am losing my mind." Until I heard the Lord say, "You are not losing your mind. I am expanding your heart."

The Lord showed me sorrow and celebration again when we met our heart donor family. My sweetheart of forty-one years (as I write this) had a heart transplant on January 28, 2020. That day was filled with lots of tears and yet lots of laughter all at the same time. We heard stories of a young man we had never met but John Mark carried his heart in his chest. Great loss and great love together.

It happened again at Easter when I read about Jesus going to the Garden of Gethsemane. The Bible records that He was singing, yet knowing what He was about to endure. Celebrating and grieving at the same time. Then the Bible says that when Mary came to the tomb, she was "afraid but filled with joy" (Matt. 28:8). Fear and joy at the same time.

Psalm 126:5–6 tells us we can sow in tears and sing with our harvest. These mixed emotions do not make us crazy, unless we do not handle them correctly and they get in the driver's seat of our life.

Last illustration, and then I am going to draw all of this to a conclusion. Earlier in the year I went to see my gynecologist. Since all types of cancer run in my family, we did a battery of tests, bloodwork, mammogram—all the things. During the evaluation, she said, "As a part of your well-woman evaluation, we now also do a checkup on your emotional and mental wellness."

Excuse me? You have poked and prodded and smashed everything on me and you want to talk about my emotional and mental state? Oh, you want to go there with me—well, knock yourself out. And she handed me a clipboard with a yellow sheet of paper in duplicate that had three short questions. She mentioned I could take mine home and she was going to put hers in my chart.

She said, "Please answer these honestly."

Question #1: Are you depressed? Circle one: Yes or No.

I feel like that should have been an easy question. I had done enough research to know that I was not clinically depressed. Depression for me was not clinical—it was situational. I guess I took too much time trying to decide my answer because she said, "Let's move on to question number two. It might be easier." But I quickly circled "No," because I had a mental need to answer all the questions.

Question #2: Are you happy or unhappy?

Again, I needed to circle one of the two … happy or unhappy. This did look a little easier because it had four emojis to choose from. I could circle the happy face emoji, the sad face emoji, the single-tear emoji, or the angry red-faced emoji. I looked at that sheet and I circled EVERY SINGLE ONE of them in big bold circles!

I am ALL of these … AT THE SAME TIME! I am happy. I am sad. I am mad at the devil, and I've cried a few tears! Can anyone relate? Can anyone say, "Girl, I get you"? You might as well add about five other emojis to this little list. You could add the shrugging emoji, the facepalm emoji, the bug-eyed one, the mind explosion one—and go ahead and throw in the cussing emoji! I cannot confirm nor deny if I have ever used it.

Why is it that our culture categorizes our feelings? Are you this or that? When things are going well, I am happy, and when they are not good, I am unhappy. It has been said of moms that we are as happy as our happiest child. I'm afraid I have fallen into that trap a time or two. But that's not what God's Word says in Jeremiah 15:16 (NASB): "Your words became a joy to me and the delight of my heart."

Things don't have to be perfect for us to be at peace.

We can have a problem and still have joy in our heart.

We can have a struggle and also have strength at the same time!

Things can be crazy, and we can still have courage.

There is purpose in our pain! We may not feel it or see it at the moment.

Where does JOY come from and how do you cultivate it? When you cultivate joy, you generate energy, peace, stability, focus, and restorative sleep. **Joy is your job!** What makes your joy complete?

> *"You make known to me the path of life; in your presence there is fullness of joy; at your right hand are pleasures forevermore" (Ps. 16:11 ESV).*

Here's a simple prayer I usually pray every day to help me stay in line with God's purpose for my life: *TEACH me what I need to know and SHOW me what I need to change.*

> *"So pay attention to how you hear. To those who listen to my teaching, more understanding will be given. But for those who are not listening, even what they think they understand will be taken away from them" (Luke 8:18 NLT).*

Joy is built into our lives as we build our lives around God's Word. And that may require a change or two.

Recently I have been working through some back **pain** issues because I don't want to have back surgery. Here's how the process went. We did some **tests**, they **revealed** some problem areas, and we came up with a **plan**, with some **practices** to correct and help. Little changes will help realign the spine and make a big difference. I changed the pillow I sleep on and now wear specific inserts in my shoes. I have a back brace to use and a certain pillow for my chair. I go to therapy, and

I do certain exercises to stretch and help eliminate pain. Little changes have made a big difference.

The Process:

- Pain
- Test
- Revelation
- Plan
- Practice

This book is not about asking you to overhaul your whole life. What God has directed us to do is to let Him reveal problem areas, then set in motion practices to correct what we can. These chapters will include tools and techniques for spiritual realignment.

Personal growth challenge: Twenty Minutes a Day for the Rest of Your Life. One thing you will hear me say over and over is: "Twenty Minutes a Day for the Rest of Your Life!" I know the Lord has called me to challenge you to spend time with Him every day. Make an appointment. Set up a place. And make it a priority. Many of us are not getting what we should be getting because we are not sitting where we should be sitting! You're welcome!

As we evaluate our lives to adjust to God's Word, let's be sure we are dealing with the real issues. For instance, we know anger is a secondary emotion. So, we must figure out what is driving the anger. Let me illustrate it this way: We have a generator at our home. Every time I drive into the driveway, I see the bright green light that lets me know that if the power goes out, this generator is coming on. Recently I drove in the driveway and saw the light was yellow. I was disturbed by this because yellow means *caution* and that there is a problem. I told my sweetheart that there was a problem with the generator! He was like, "Let me call the guy." (He has a guy for everything. If something happens to my sweetheart I am in a lot of trouble because I don't know who the guys are. We have a bug guy, a car guy, a yard guy, and so forth.)

Anyway, a few days later, I noticed the light was green again. And I said to John Mark, "Oh, I am so glad you got the generator problem fixed!" He said, "We didn't have a generator problem." I replied, "Umm, I'm pretty sure we did. I saw the yellow light that indicated there was a problem." (I may or may not have said this with a Southern attitude and the flip of my hair.) He said we didn't have a generator problem; we had a wasp problem! Wasps had built a huge nest on the control panel, which caused the yellow caution light. Something was not working right. Now, flip that to the spiritual side. The yellow light was letting us know there was a problem alright, but it was not the problem we thought it was by looking at the outside. Let's take a look at the inside. Something may have gotten out of whack in our spiritual or emotional control panel. Like the wasps got in the generator, disturbances get in our minds.

How do we fix it?

Get in His presence! The Bible says in Psalm 16:11 (ESV), "You make known to me the path of life; in your presence there is fullness of joy; at your right hand are pleasures forevermore." It doesn't say that in His presence there is a problem in our life.

We must position ourselves with the Lord and make room for Him to work.

Proverbs 2:10 (NLT) says, "For wisdom will enter your heart, and knowledge will fill you with joy."

Psalm 34:5 (NLT) says, "Those who look to him for help will be radiant with joy." A grateful heart is a stable heart.

In John 15:11 (ESV), Jesus says, "These things I have spoken to you, that my joy may be in you, and that your joy may be full." When did He speak and what things did He say? God speaks when we spend time with Him in His Word.

John 15:1–10 (NKJV) is the passage where God says, "I am the vine, you are the branches. He who abides in Me, and I in him, bears much fruit; for without Me you can do nothing."

Two things that will make your joy full are: ABIDE and REMAIN.

- **Abide** is to continue to be present, to dwell with constant connection.
- **Remain** is to endure, persevere, and not leave.

These are choices we make every day. Recently I read a quote by a Holocaust survivor. Their name was not given, but they made an important point: "Between stimulus and response there is a space. In that space is our power to choose our response. In our response lies our growth and our freedom." When something happens to us, we choose our response to it. And that choice will set things in motion.

We enjoy keeping grandkids in our home. Recently, our youngest, Gunner (age three at the time), was spending the day at my house. We were playing outside, and I have lots of plants. He noticed the impatiens with pink flowers and pulled one off. I am not sure what feelings that produced in him. But he liked it. So, he pulled off another one and was going for the next one when I said, "Gunner, NO. Do not pull my flowers." He looked back at me and looked back at those flowers (apparently, they were begging him to pull them), and he yanked another one off, this time with a little more force. He liked what he was doing. He felt like he was in charge. But I popped his little hand and said NO, which I had never done before. That moment WAS HIS SPACE—the time to choose his response. Between stimulus and response, there is a space.

It was the little time between stimuli, what just happened to him, and how he would respond. He's a sweet little boy; I am sure he hasn't had his hand popped many times and he wasn't sure how he wanted to respond. I wish you could have seen the look on his face.

Oh, I could see what was going on in his little mind. I could tell part of him wanted:

- To pull one more flower—as if to say, "I'm going to do what I want to do."
- To pop my hand right back.
- To cry because he got his feelings hurt.

But do you know what he did? I was quite surprised by it. He withheld affection from me, because he knows that's what Dodie loves the most. He walked away. And he would not come to me.

I'm going to let that sit with you for a minute as we look to the spiritual part of our lives.

What has happened or hurt you in your life? How did you respond? Have you walked away because you got your feelings hurt?

I know what some of you are thinking because I have thought it and felt the same thing: *Debbie, you don't know what's going on in my life right now. I am hurting and it is not a joyful time. Things are hard and I'm brokenhearted. And you are saying, "Choose joy!" "Choose joy" sounds like an empty cliché to me.* I get that! Let me help you.

You can be FORCED into a situation you did not want to be in and still have fullness of joy at the same time. BECAUSE that situation does not dictate nor does it control your joy.

We find Paul and Silas in jail according to Acts 16, and the Bible says they had been beaten severely, put in the inner dungeon, and shackled to the stocks. Then the Bible records that they were *singing hymns and praising God.* Let me ask you a question: Were they hurting? YES! But they chose to sing hymns and praise the Lord AT THE SAME TIME they were hurting.

Remember the song "Raise a Hallelujah" by Bethel Music? One verse says: "My weapon is a melody."[1]

The enemy wants us *hurting, confused, disengaged, stressed out,* and *worried.* He wants us *unproductive* and *ineffective* in the things of God. He loves to exaggerate the situation. He loves to cause doubt and fear. He doesn't want us singing hymns and praising God. But you have a choice: Choose JOY!

---

[1] Jonathan David Helser and Melissa Helser, "Raise a Hallelujah," *Victory*, Bethel Music Publishing, 2019.

I keep this poem by Lettie B. Cowman in my Bible and refer to it often:

> He placed me in a little cage, away from gardens fair
> But I must sing the sweetest songs, because He placed me there
> Not beat my wings against the cage
> If it's my maker's will
> But raise my voice to heaven's gate and sing the louder still.[2]

The Bible says if you ABIDE and REMAIN—you will cultivate joy!

"I have told you these things, so that in me you may have peace. In this world you will have trouble. But take heart! I have overcome the world" (John 16:33).

- He gives peace but you will have trouble,
- Struggles AND strength,
- Burdens AND blessings,
- Adversity but also have the advantage,
- Craziness AND courage.

We can have a beautiful disaster. We can have a successful shipwreck.

We can feel like we are sinking but we can sing at the same time!

> *What joy for those whose strength comes from the Lord, who have set their minds on a pilgrimage to Jerusalem. When they walk through the Valley of Weeping, it will become a place of refreshing springs. The autumn rains will clothe it with blessings. (Psalm 84:5–6 NLT)*

WHEN ... not AFTER they walk through ... and not IF. The Valley of Weeping and refreshing springs AT THE SAME TIME!

Hosea 2:15 (NLT) says, "I will ... transform the Valley of Trouble into a gateway of hope." You can have bright and beautiful AT THE SAME TIME the Lord asks you to carry dark and disappointing. Our natural tendency is to be one or the other. It's either bright and beautiful or dark and disappointing. Hey, darlin', you've been chosen for this ... not cheated because of it.

---

2   Lettie B. Cowman, *Streams in the Desert: 366 Daily Devotional Readings* (Zondervan, 1999).

Psalm 126:6 (NLT) says, "They weep as they go to plant their seed, but they sing as they return with the harvest."

There is sorrow but there is singing!

Jeremiah 31:25 (NLT) says, "For I have given rest to the weary and joy to the sorrowing."

Philippians 4:4 (ESV) is a must to memorize! Does it say, "Rejoice in the Lord *sometimes*"? No, it says: "Rejoice in the Lord always; again I will say …" what? Rejoice! Always be full of joy in the Lord.

Honest evaluation: What have you been full of? Fear, attitude, fatigue, anger, frustration, anxiety? Take a moment to pray about it and ask the Lord to fill you with the opposite emotion. From fear to peace. From fatigue to energy. From anger and frustration to joy.

In gardening I've learned the good stuff has to be cultivated. The bad stuff pops up automatically. I must be intentional if I want squash and tomatoes. But weeds, vines, poison ivy, and fungus pop up automatically. And if I don't get them out, they will take over and kill the good stuff.

Read James 1:2–4. Dear sisters, when trouble comes your way, consider it an opportunity for whining and complaining? No, it says to consider it GREAT JOY. For you know that WHEN your faith is tested, your endurance has a chance to grow. So, let it grow. Trials and troubles should be an opportunity for joy; they help us grow, persevere, and develop endurance.

Habakkuk 3:18 (NLT) says, "I will be joyful in the God of my salvation!"

Nehemiah 8:10 (NLT) says, "For the joy of the LORD is your strength."

CHOOSE JOY! Practice joy!

> *"She is clothed with strength and dignity, and she laughs without fear of the future"* (Prov. 31:25 NLT).

Focus Verse

"Dear brothers and sisters, when troubles of any kind come your way, consider it an opportunity for great joy. For you know that when your faith is tested, your endurance has a chance to grow. So let it grow, for when your endurance is fully developed, you will be perfect and complete, needing nothing" (Jas. 1:2–4 NLT).

Connecting the Dots

The focus verse has many verbs requiring mental action with the primary noun being joy.

- **Trouble** includes difficulty, problems, tests, and temptations.
- **Joy** is pleasure, delight, and according to Strong's Concordance, a "calm delight."[3]
- **Endurance** is defined as the ability to withstand hardship or adversity.
- **To consider** is to let joy rule over your trouble and to think carefully before making decisions.

Make It Personal

Let's take a moment for some honest evaluation. How would you finish this sentence? *When trouble comes my way, it is an opportunity for me to*

_____

_____

_____

_____

_____ .

---

3   James Strong, *Strong's Expanded Exhaustive Concordance of the Bible* (Thomas Nelson, 2009), s. v. "joy."

How can we be sure that God has us occupied with gladness of heart? (See Acts 13:52.)

_____

_____

_____

_____

What exactly are our hearts and minds occupied with, and how can we fill our minds with answers to overcome what is troubling us? (See Matthew 22:37; Romans 8:6; Psalm 92:4.)

_____

_____

_____

_____

SUMMARY

> *"And it is a good thing to receive wealth from God and the good health to enjoy it. To enjoy your work and accept your lot in life—this is indeed a gift from God" (Eccles. 5:19 NLT).*

> *"They seldom reflect on the days of their life, because God keeps them occupied with gladness of heart" (Eccles. 5:20).*

Let's break this down a bit for deeper understanding and personal application.

What does it even mean to accept your "lot in life"? It means to accept your assignments from the Lord—the good, the bad, the hard, the easy, the fun, and ALL He has allowed. We accept it knowing He is working all things out for our good. Why? Because we love Him and are called according to His purpose (see Romans 8:28).

What do we "reflect on" (focus on)? What is our mind set on? I love the part that says, "They seldom reflect on the days of their life," which means they don't keep looking back with regret and sadness and wishing their life was different, BECAUSE God keeps them occupied with gladness and joy of heart!

My prayer is that you have been filled with greater joy!

Now, go live your best life filled with JOY!

Chapter Three

Don't. Do. Nothing!

*"The eyes of the LORD search the whole earth in order to
strengthen those whose hearts are fully committed to him."*
2 Chronicles 16:9 (NLT)

Divine assignments and defining moments are available for us in the
coming year. That is why I am anxious to share an important message
the Lord has been building in me. It's a spiritual lesson that must be
implemented in our lives if we are going to finish strong. I am well into
the last half of my life and there are three words from this story in the
Bible that have significantly impacted my perspective and altered the
trajectory of my life.

While I was on a six-week spiritual study sabbatical, some interesting
things happened. The Lord led me to three messages from His Word:

- A message of remembrance—something He wanted me to
  remember.
- A message of revelation—something I needed to know.
- A message of caution—a fairly serious caution, which I want
  to share with you.

Grab your Bible and turn to 2 Chronicles 16.

During this study sabbatical, I was preparing for an upcoming Bible
study called *Fully Devoted*. What does it look like in our lives, and what
are the best practices of a person who is fully devoted? (Refer to your
answers in chapter one if you need a refresher.) From the beginning, I

thought about the verse in 2 Chronicles 16:9 (ESV): "For the eyes of the LORD run to and fro throughout the whole earth, to give strong support to those whose heart is blameless toward him."

The Message Bible paraphrases it like this: "You asked God for help and he gave you the victory. God is always on the alert, constantly on the lookout for people who are totally committed to him." He is overly attentive to those who are fully devoted.

Being sensitive to the Lord's prompting, and before we begin looking at this story, would you please set your heart to hear from the Lord? We want to learn what it means for our lives too. Remove any obstacles of communication and decide right now that you will be responsive to the Lord. This message may not be what you want to hear but I truly believe it's one we all need to hear.

Set your heart to hear from the Lord.

When we look at 2 Chronicles 16:9, we see that the Lord puts His strength into people who are fully devoted to Him. When I read it, I couldn't help but wonder, *Hmm, what happened in verses 1–8 to cause the Lord to say this in verse 9?* See, this is why you should never jerk a verse out of context. You have to read the Scriptures associated with it. And, girl, there is a story that the Lord wants us to know about. So, buckle up, buttercup—it's a wild ride and it is a cautionary tale that has important implications for us.

The Chronicles are given in God's Word not only to provide historical records, but also to serve for us as examples, warnings, and cautions for our lives.

This chapter is the story of King Asa. Let me give you the background:

- He was a king that ruled over Judah, and he was in his thirty-sixth year of being king.
- The Bible records that Asa did what was good and right in the eyes of the Lord. For thirty-five years, he was devoted to the Lord and the things of God and the direction of God.

- Asa's name means "God is my physician." Oh, the irony in that! Hang on to that because we are coming back to it.

The Bible, in my NLT translation, lists twenty-two things that Asa did right. Over and over, he did as the Lord instructed. Even at times against great opposition. I mean, he was kickin' it! The Lord had said, "No idols! You must destroy all the idols! Stop worshiping other things. Devote yourself to Me. Please just worship Me and commit your life to Me." For us, that translates to: What is taking up so much of our time and attention? *Hint: It's a three-by-five-inch device and has a camera in it.*

So, Asa did as the Lord instructed. The problem was his mother and his grandmother worshiped idols, in a big way. It takes a determined, strong person to go against Mamma and Memaw!

My mother-in-law, affectionately known as "Memi," was our only living parent until February 12, 2025, when she stepped into heaven one day before her ninetieth birthday. She was the matriarch of our family. As we studied the story of Asa, we were spending the holidays with her. She was a godly woman, a feisty woman, a widow, and not even five feet tall—did I mention she was feisty?

The deal is, we let her do what she wanted to do. Sometimes we didn't agree, but we would say, "Just let her have what she wants and to do it her way." She made some ridiculous requests. She had a two-page grocery list every week and she did not cook anything. But we gave her what she wanted. We were like, "She's ninety. Just let her do it." (Anybody know what I am talking about?) And if you don't know, you're probably the one everybody says that about!

But Asa was being completely obedient to the Lord. He made Mamma and Memaw get with the program. He did not care how old they were or what their personal preferences were. Biblical note: Your age is not permission, nor a reason, to do your own thing.

Let's read what happened in 2 Chronicles 16:1–9. Let me paraphrase:

- Asa had been seeking the Lord for guidance about battles and the Lord had been delivering him and his people for years.

- In year thirty-six, he stopped seeking he Lord. He underhandedly went and bought protection (made a deal with) a heathen king. He was trying to serve his personal preferences.
- The Lord sent the prophet Hanani to confront him, and he told him, "You are not loyal to the Lord. You did not do what was right." Hanani was setting him up for correction and repentance. But that didn't happen. Instead, Asa threw Hanani into prison and tortured him.
- Then he contracted a debilitating foot disease, and the Bible records he refused to seek the Lord's help. He only sought help from others. Remember what Asa's name means? It means "God is my physician." Really, Asa, you stopped all communication with the Lord. Why?

Let me put that in today's language. After thirty-six years of walking with the Lord, **he ghosted God!** If you are not familiar with that term, it means to suddenly cut off communication and drop out of someone's life.

He had been following the Lord for thirty-six years. What happened? Why the change of heart? Why the sudden shift in behavior and mindset? He was a seasoned leader who had walked with the Lord for a long time.

What happened? I just had to know. I started looking and researching for some reason, something that happened causing him a temporary loss of judgment. Why would he walk away from the Lord? I looked for something that caused a lapse in his spiritual journey, a momentary "I lost my mind for a minute," because of something that happened.

I thought about my own life and times when I got sidetracked with the Lord, or more honestly, when I got sideways with the Lord. I've been in ministry for over thirty-three years at this point and I've seen many times when this has happened in the lives of women: When a loved one was taken. When a cancer diagnosis came. When there was an unexpected divorce, a job loss, a prodigal child, an addicted husband, an insecurity, loneliness, loss, betrayal, hurt—all of these things can get us off track.

Asa's story is one of a splendid beginning and a tragic ending. It holds great life lessons for us. God had given him great victories and used him in great ways. He was loyal and listened to God. He obeyed His direction. He communicated with God regularly … until he didn't.

So, what happened? What happened to him and what happens to us?

I discovered exactly what happened and what caused him to neglect his time with the Lord. God's Word revealed why he no longer made meeting and talking with the Lord a priority in his life.

The answer: Nothing! Nothing happened! There was no crisis, no hardship, no difficulty to work through. He did nothing to continue his walk with the Lord.

- He stopped relying on the Lord.
- He did what HE wanted to do. He worked HIS plan.
- He had his own agenda.
- He didn't listen to correction.
- He failed to correct himself.
- His heart was not loyal.
- He didn't humble himself.
- He failed to obey God.
- He sought only human solutions to problems.
- He was stubborn.
- He was non-reliant on the Lord.
- He was no longer responsive to the word of the Lord.
- And worst of all, he resisted the word of the Lord.

Here's an important principle I've learned: Prolonged non-reliance on the Lord causes ongoing resistance to the Lord.

He was faithful … until he wasn't!

Things changed for Asa in the final years of his life, and he did not finish strong.

We will never outgrow our ability to sin! It's been suggested that the older we get the more self-centered we become. Past spiritual victory does not guarantee future spiritual success. Committing oneself to God's agenda is a DAY-BY-DAY experience—a choice we make every day (Twenty Minutes a Day for the Rest of Your Life).

We will never be so spiritually mature that we cannot get off track. And we can go from disciplined to "diva" in a very short period of time.

EXAMPLES

Noah was a mature man when he got drunk. Abraham had been following the Lord for years when he got off track and lied about his wife. Moses was a seasoned leader when he lost his temper. David committed his life to the Lord until his own personal desires wrecked his life. We could name well-known leaders in our society who, after serving the Lord for thirty to forty years, had to leave ministry in a cloud of scandal, suspicion, or criminal action.

Asa changed in his attitudes and actions during those last years. Apparently, Asa had become complacent during those days, and he made a change from being committed to being noncommitted. Asa's attitude was offensive to the Lord. He made decisions that caused spiritual decline and ultimate failure.

God tried to correct his behavior by sending someone to speak truth into his life. Instead of repentance before the Lord, he refused to humble himself before the Lord. These decisions marred his legacy. He refused to say, "I'm sorry, Lord. I lost my way. Please forgive me." Perhaps because something happened or because nothing happened.

The three words from this story that wrecked my world are: **Don't. Do. Nothing!**

Don't do nothing regarding your spiritual life. And don't get busy doing nothing.

What happened to Asa? Nothing happened. He did nothing to express his devotion to the Lord. He did nothing to show obedience and faithfulness. He no longer felt the pull to get with the Lord every day. He neglected his twenty minutes a day with the Lord. It is imperative that you meet with the Lord daily. Set up a place to meet with the Lord in solitude and He will meet you there.

He was fully devoted … until he wasn't! Of the many kings listed in 2 Chronicles, only six were recorded as serving the Lord with their whole heart.

Therefore, this is the time for honest self-evaluation. What's your mind thinking about? What direction are you moving? What are you doing? Any lights flashing on the dashboard?

Let's look at warning signs—caution lights we need to pay attention to.

Here's a CAUTION LIST. Ask the Lord if any of these are problem areas for you:

C Careless with time, complacent in attitude, comfortable, self-centered
A Absent from spending time with the Lord, attitude problem
U Unwilling to self-correct, unfaithful to the Lord, unteachable
T Taking matters into your own hands, trying to fix things yourself
I Ignoring God's Word, ignorant, impatient, insisting on your way
O Obstinate, opposed to God, overlooking blessings, an offended heart
N Neglecting your spiritual life, not following God's agenda and instructions

Surrender your agenda! Don't have prolonged resistance to the Lord!

I was listening to a news anchor talk about what seems to be a shift in New Year's resolutions. A new thing has emerged at the first of the year: You don't do resolutions. He interviewed person after person that said, "I'm not doing anything. I don't feel like making any changes." People were proud to have NO New Year's resolutions. I'm not sure that's a good thing.

I'm not asking you to overhaul your whole life. I'm asking us all to take a hard look at what we are doing with our time, our experiences, and our skills. Are we doing things that are spiritually productive, emotionally healthy, and make us mentally strong?

I hope we agree: Don't. Do. Nothing.

What one thing can we do to get us started on our journey to knowing God better and making His Word the priority in our life?

One thing: Water the seed (God's Word) that has been planted in your life with this message. How do you do that? You get with the Lord every day and in Bible study every week. The Bible says, "Planted in the house of the LORD, they will flourish in the courts of our God" (Ps. 92:13).

> **Water the seed (God's Word) that has been planted in your life.**

For overachievers, I'll give you one more thing. Ask the Lord for a word for this year—something He wants you to focus on or develop. Perhaps there is something the Lord wants to build in your life that you are not yet aware of.

I have a sweet, young gal in my life, and we have been talking about the concept of "a word of the year." When I asked her about her word, she said, "I'm not doing that. I'm not getting on that bandwagon." I'll tell you what I told her: "I see your social media. I've seen you on a lot of other bandwagons you don't need to be on so why not jump on one that will help you?"

Remember our caution list. Caution: Do not neglect God's Word (or a word of the year from the Lord).

DON'T. DO. NOTHING!

Don't act out, step out, tap out, bail out, or give out!

Some of you have been riding in the boat for a long time. It's time to start rowing the boat!

Focus Verse

"For the eyes of the LORD roam throughout the earth to show himself strong for those whose who are wholeheartedly devoted to him" (2 Chron. 16:9 CSB).

Connecting the Dots

How do you see Asa's last years of life comparing to our focus verse?

_____

_____

_____

Memorizing this verse will be helpful to keep us on track when tempted to turn our backs on God and His Word.

Make It Personal

Look up the verses below that counter the statements in the CAUTION acrostic. Write in your own words how they will help us to be cautious from falling away from the Lord.

C – Titus 3:7; Proverbs 4:1; 1 Timothy 4:15

_____

_____

_____

A – Numbers 14:24; Philippians 2:5; 1 Peter 3:8

_____

_____

_____

U – Acts 11:23; Psalm 25:4–5

_____

_____

_____

T – Psalm 37:5; Matthew 6:6

_____

_____

_____

I – Romans 12:12; 1 Corinthians 13:4; Jeremiah 29:13

_____

_____

_____

O – Mark 4:20; Psalm 119:35

_____

_____

_____

N – 1 Peter 4:1–2; 1 John 2:7

_____

_____

_____

SUMMARY

Have a soft heart toward things of the Lord. Listen to Him, seek Him, and surrender your will to God's plan and His will for you.

Chapter Four

Full Life in Empty Places

"I'll give you a full life in the emptiest of places."
Isaiah 58:12 (MSG)

Our focus verse for this chapter is one the Lord led me to when I was twenty-three and had a five-week-old baby boy named Jarrad. It was about four a.m. I was feeding him and crying as I did. My mom was forty when she lost a courageous battle with aggressive cancer, and we had just buried her. We begged God to heal her. If tears could have saved someone, she would be alive today! I was exhausted and depleted. I. Was. Empty.

I knew I was headed to a bad place emotionally, mentally, and spiritually. Honestly, I was a little mad at the Lord. Okay … more than a little. But I knew how to get it turned around. I had to get in God's Word. If I wanted to "get out of my head," I had to get in His Word. So, I opened my Bible.

In my dark, depleted place, God's Word reminded me: "The unfolding of your words gives light; it gives understanding to the simple" (Ps. 119:130). And, "Your word is a lamp for my feet and a light on my path" (Ps. 119:105 CSB).

Darlin', you don't have to be in a dark place. I didn't say you don't have to be in a hard place. We will talk about that in another chapter.

God's Word gives us light. Not like a runway, which lights up for miles and is preferred. Sometimes, it is just enough light for the step we are on. But it is light, nonetheless.

I miss my relationship with my mom terribly. She always pointed me in the right direction, encouraged me in God's Word, and tried to explain things I did not understand. She's been gone many years. In her absence I found myself wishing someone had told me some things … about life, grief, relationships, emotions, sons and daughters, and how the Lord works in all of it to accomplish His plan and purpose for my life. I've had the hardest time trying to figure out when to hold on and when to let go—when to step out in faith and when to wait. I didn't know how to carry sorrow very well. I've thought, *I don't know what I need to know,* and, *Somebody should have said something.*

> **I developed the habit of spending time with the Lord**

"Somebody should have said something" is a phrase I would like to shout from the mountaintop! When we've been through something—when we've had some experiences and learned a lesson or two—we must tell somebody. It is part of our testimony of how God works in our lives. That we may be mutually encouraged *and* comforted by each other's faith, both yours and mine (see Romans 1:12).

For a long time in my life, I took two steps forward and one step back in my walk with the Lord. I wasted a lot of time that way. I didn't really know what I was doing. I wish somebody would have said something! So, I want to be one that will step up and say something based on some truths I have learned in God's Word.

Through the various stages of life, especially the one I'm in (I'm sixty this year), I've been a little shocked at the weird things that are happening to me. I have discovered in this season that my mind and my body no longer agree on things! My mind would like to do things that my body refuses to participate in. Every evening my mind would like my body to get on the exercise bike, yet my body, in full blown rebellion of this idea, stands firmly planted in the kitchen eating a brownie. My mind says, "You should not be doing that; you should be exercising." My body responds with, "Keep talking and I will eat this whole pan of brownies!" I feel like there are two different people in my mind (sometimes more!) and nobody told me about this. I think if I am going to routinely stick my head in the freezer compartment of my fridge, somebody should have said something! Last winter it snowed five to six inches, and we had a hard freeze. I stood outside in shorts and said, "This feels awesome!" Again, a little heads up on the craziest happenings would have been nice.

So, spending time in God's Word every day has saved my ever-lovin' life. Well, actually Christ dying on the cross is what saved me. When I developed the habit of spending time with the Lord, it saved my mind from going crazy. (And believe me when I say I come from a long line of wackadoos, so there is a propensity for crazy!) It saved my emotions from driving me to dark places, and it saved me from believing every lie the enemy tried to tell me.

I want us to *learn* God's Word and *apply* God's Word to our lives. Let's stop trying to figure out everything on our own, "playing church," and telling everyone we're "FINE!" Don't hide in your sin and don't hide in your sorrow.

First Kings 18:21 (ESV) asks an important question: "How long will you go limping between two different opinions? If the LORD is God, follow him."

What if every Bible study workbook fell off the face of the earth—would we be okay? Do we know what to do with our Bible and a clean sheet of paper? Can we hear Him speak and pull out biblical principles to live by?

Let me explain further, please. Turn in your Bible to Joshua chapter 1.

Read verses 1–9. Moses, the leader of God's people, had died, and God called up the next leader, Joshua. Beginning in verse 7, we are given the keys to a successful life:

> *Be strong and very courageous. Be careful to obey all the instructions Moses gave you. Do not deviate from them, turning either to the right or to the left. Then you will be successful in everything you do. Study this Book of Instruction continually. Meditate on it day and night so you will be sure to obey everything written in it. Only then will you prosper and succeed in all you do. This is my command—be strong and courageous! Do not be afraid or discouraged. For the LORD your God is with you wherever you go. (Joshua 1:7–9)*

The Lord tells us exactly what to do to have success in life. From the verses in this chapter, take a moment to jot down the action words from the verses. Define them. Look up synonyms and antonyms to those words. Why? Because we can sometimes find ourselves doing the opposite of what God directs us to do.

ACTION WORDS	DEFINED	SYNONYMS	ANTONYMS

We must be in the Word every day and not depart from it. Don't turn to the right or to the left. That's it.

Nothing more. Nothing less. Nothing else.

I like to say it this way: "Twenty Minutes a Day for the Rest of Your Life!"

The power of God at work in our lives is dependent upon our relationship and communication with Him. We develop our relationship and deepen our communication with Him by spending time with Him in His Word. The written Word is health to our spiritual bones, giving us insight and better focus to see the vision God has for not only our lives but for the day at hand. The more we saturate ourselves in the Scriptures, the easier it becomes for the power of God to work in our lives and become useful to His kingdom purposes. It cleanses us from wrong desires and clears away our own thoughts and connects us to God's desires and thoughts.

So, the challenge is on the table: Twenty Minutes a Day for the Rest of Your Life! I pray you will accept it.

Psalm 1:2 (MSG) says, "You THRILL to God's Word, you chew on Scripture day and night" (emphasis mine). Let's ask the Lord to cause us to "thrill to God's Word" and ask Him to point out any hindrances or unhealthy relationship that keep us from spiritual progress.

In the book *Switch On Your Brain* by Dr. Caroline Leaf, she makes this statement after a research project: "It has been found that twelve minutes of daily focused prayer over an eight-week period can change the brain to such an extent that it can be measured on a brain scan."[4]

We can change our brain! We can train our brain by spending time in God's Word every day.

> *"The people who know their God will be strong and take action" (Dan. 11:32 CSB).*

It is absolutely essential to spend time with the Lord! No excuses.

We **will not** know Him, His will, or His ways apart from His Word!

We don't need to fill in the blanks in a workbook to hear Him speak. Let's stop with the "feed me" mentality and let's learn to feed ourselves!

> *"You were running well. Who hindered you from obeying the truth? This persuasion is not from him who calls you" (Gal. 5:7–8 ESV).*

> *"You were running a good race. Who cut in on you to keep you from obeying the truth?" (Gal. 5:7).*

---

4   Dr. Caroline Leaf, *Switch On Your Brain: The Key to Peak Happiness, Thinking, and Health* (Baker Books, 2013).

Maybe a person "cut in on you." A name might be coming to your mind right now. If not, surely a name of another kind: cancer, betrayal, adultery, infertility, bankruptcy, anger, loneliness, laziness, regret—oh, how they can hinder our progress!

Focus Verse

"I'll give you a full life in the emptiest of places" (Isa. 58:11 MSG).

Twenty Minutes a Day for the Rest of Your Life positions us for the Lord to give us a full life in the emptiest of places. Some of us are not getting what we should be getting, because we are not sitting where we should be sitting. You're welcome!

Connecting the Dots

What are the hindrances to receiving this full life in the emptiest places that our focus verse speaks of? Examine your heart as you read the helpful hints below to determine if any apply to you.

_____

_____

_____

_____

_____

Helpful Hints to Apply God's Word to Your Life

Below are application questions to ask the Lord during your study. Then sit still. Be quiet. Let the Lord answer in your spirit and give direction to your heart. Respond to Him. What will you do as a result of what He has said and shown you? Answer *yes, no, maybe,* or *I need to work in this area.* It is also helpful to record this experience in your journal.

A	Is there an **A**ttitude I need to adjust?
P	Is there a **P**romise I need to claim?
P	Is there a **P**riority I need to change?
L	Is there a **L**esson I need to learn?
I	Is there an **I**ssue I need to resolve?
C	Is there a **C**ommand I need to obey?
A	Is there an **A**ctivity I need to avoid?
T	Is there a **T**ruth I need to believe?
I	Is there an **I**dol I need to tear down?
O	Is there an **O**ffense I need to forgive?
N	Is there a **N**ew direction I need to take?
S	Is there a **S**in I need to confess?

Make It Personal

How would your life change if you spent twenty minutes a day with the Lord for the rest of your life?

_____

_____

_____

Do you have a clear sense of God's purpose for your life?

_____

_____

_____

Does the concept of training your brain by reading and studying God's Word excite you or discourage you? Why or why not?

_____

_____

_____

SUMMARY

I'm referring back to my story at the beginning of this chapter to encourage you with knowing no matter what we go through, God is with us. He never leaves us to face our difficulties alone. He hears us when we cry out to Him. God proves what He will do for us through His Word. Read the following verses and pray them back to the Lord with a thankful heart for all He is and all He does for us.

- "Morning by morning he wakens me and opens my understanding to his will" (Isa. 50:4 NLT).
- "My heart has heard you say, 'Come and talk with me.' And my heart responds, 'LORD, I am coming'" (Ps. 27:8 NLT).
- "I will search for faithful people to be my companions" (Ps. 101:6 NLT).
- "Be still in the presence of the LORD" (Ps. 37:7 NLT).
- "Blessed is the one who listens to me, watching daily at my gates, waiting beside my doors" (Prov. 8:34 ESV).
- "Strengthen me according to your word!" (Ps. 119:28 ESV).
- "The Lord gives the word; the women who announce the good news are a great host" (Ps. 68:11 ESV).

Chapter Five

Doorways and Decisions

"'Call her.' So he called her, and she stood in the doorway."
2 Kings 4:15

There is a story in God's Word about a woman and a doorway. Her name is not given, but her legacy of faith has lived on for many centuries. I see myself and my life circumstances play out in a similar way and this story in God's Word helps me make the right decisions when things go wrong. The Lord has some important life lessons for us in this woman's story. There are seven lessons to be exact.

Her story is found in 2 Kings 4:8–37. I hope you will take a few minutes to read the story, then read further for some important details. Ask the Lord to give you personal insight and help you see some spiritual observations.

This is the story of the Shunammite woman. She was given that name because she lived in the town of Shunem. The Bible tells us important details about her and about what was going on in her life. One translation refers to her as a great woman.

Now that you have read the story:

- What stands out to you?
- What interesting facts did you notice in the story?
- What part of this story was meaningful to you?

I relate to her on so many levels! Her experience grabbed my attention and is so meaningful. The Lord caused me to picture myself (like her) standing in the doorway—like, not going ALL IN, but just going to stand there and see what The Lord has to say. Think about it for a moment. Picture it.

"So he called her, and she stood in the doorway" (2 Kings 4:15).

When we are in a doorway, we have not yet decided to "go in." We could easily make the decision to "go on by." Doors in the Bible serve both literal and figurative purposes, often symbolizing opportunities, boundaries, and access to God. They represent decisions, transitions and the choices that shape our destinies.

> **"So he called her, and she stood in the doorway" (2 Kings 4:15).**

She made a decision in the doorway that changed her entire life. It set her up for a miracle. God blessed her decision to go ALL IN! No doubt the Lord has brought us to "doorways" in our lives that require us to go ALL IN! But a decision must be made at that critical moment. And make no mistake—no decision is still a decision.

Characteristics of the Woman God Called To in the Doorway:

Here's what we learn about her (ask the Lord to help you apply this to your life):

1. **She was *discerning*.** We know this because the Bible says she "perceived" Elisha to be a holy man of God. She *saw* God at work (which required eyes of faith), and she wanted to be involved in that work. Her ministry, she decided, would be to support this man called of God. She lifted his burden, made his work easier, and she provided comfort, rest, and fellowship.

We learn from Henry Blackaby in his book *Experiencing God*: "See where God is working in your world—and join Him in that work."[5]

2. **She *served* others** and she *shared* what she had. She used her gift of hospitality. What I particularly like about her preparing a room for Elisha is God's attention to detail which was listed in the story. "Let's build a small room for him on the roof and furnish it with a bed, a table, a chair, and a lamp" (2 Kings 4:10 NLT). In my humble estimation, this proves that Hobby Lobby is of the Lord! The Lord made sure these little helpful accessories were listed in the Bible. I love it!

What did she do next?

3. **She *made room*!** She made room in her life for what God was doing.

Important application: Make room in your life for the Lord!

She created space for the things of God. Her priorities shifted. We make room for what's important in our lives. You may be thinking, "Make room? What does that even mean?" Let me illustrate: Before my grandkids came into my life, my life was very full. My calendar, house, schedule, and budget were all full. But when Clark Andrew Taylor was given to me, I made room! Yes, ma'am, Dodie (that's my grandmother name) made lots of room. I made room on my calendar; I made a place in my house and on my schedule. And you know I made room in my budget! I told Skeeter (that's John Mark's grandfather name), "I'm going to need some money, and lots of it!" See how we make room for what is important to us?

What God was doing in the life of the Shunammite woman became more important than what she was doing. She used what she had. She was generous. "She did what she could".

4. **She was *content*.** When she was asked what they could do for her, she did not give a long list of all the things she wanted.

5   Henry Blackaby and Claude V. King, *Experiencing God: Knowing and Doing the Will of God* (Lifeway Press, 2009).

She didn't take advantage of the situation. She basically said, "I'm good." But was she?

Elisha asked his servant Gehazi what he thought they could do for her. The servant said, "She has no son" (2 Kings 4:14).

And that brings her to the doorway.

As I picture this scenario, I think of infertility in our own family. My daughter has experienced three miscarriages and one infant loss. It is a painful journey and sorrow comes in waves, often unexpected. To be completely honest, if I were her and I was asked, "What can I do for you?" I would have shouted, "Please give us a baby! We long to have a child."

Let me tread lightly here. I am aware of the tenderness of a broken heart. However, please notice her response of contentment reveals that her barrenness (personal suffering) had not stifled her willingness to serve others. She didn't curl up in her own room; she instead made room for others and made room for God to work. I certainly don't want to deny that there are some seasons of suffering when we are unable to serve others, but I do want her selflessness to be true of me even in times of pain.

She dared to believe.

In the doorway she was told she would have a baby.

Her response inspires me. She wanted to believe but her mind raced to try to figure out if this could really be happening. Had a miracle just occurred in the doorway? She dared to believe.

"And blessed is she who believed that there would be a fulfillment of what was spoken to her from the Lord" (Luke 1:45 ESV).

I believe she made an important decision standing there that day, in the doorway. She decided to believe God! She went all in, and she had a baby!

But I was shocked at the tragic turn of events the Bible records happened next:

> *The child grew, and one day he went out to his father, who was with the reapers. He said to his father, "My head! My head!" His father told a servant, "Carry him to his mother." After the servant had lifted him up and carried him to his mother, the boy sat on her lap until noon, and then he died. (2 Kings 4:18–20 NIV)*

Wait just a dang minute. I'm sorry, WHAT!?! The child died! Why? Why would God allow that?

I'm glad you asked. Let's look for some answers in what happened next. And please, let me just say that I do not mean to diminish anything that has happened in your life. But I have learned that often it's not what happened that is so important, but it's what happens NEXT that is so important!

The Bible records what she did next. I'm paraphrasing the next part of the story, but please, take time to read this story for yourself.

Step one: She laid him on the bed of the man of God and shut the door.

Note: She laid him in the space she created for the Lord's work.

Think on that for a moment.

Step two: She asked her husband for a donkey so she could go see the man of God.

Her husband asked her if everything was okay. And she said yes, everything was okay.

Question: Was everything okay? No, it was not.

Let's chase this part of the story for a moment. I believe it carries a helpful observation on WHY she did WHAT she did. I wondered why she lied to her husband. Why didn't she tell him what happened to his son? After some study time and asking the Lord for insight, this is my personal opinion (it's not a newsflash from heaven). She kept this matter between HER and HER Lord. She didn't make it between her and her husband. He didn't give her this child. She knew he came from the Lord. And she was going right back to the Lord regarding him. This is a great practice for us. Sometimes we make things, issues, and experiences between us and someone else when we should keep them between ourselves and the Lord.

Let's get back to our list of this woman's characteristics:

5. **She was *focused*.** She remained calm and did not panic. She knew she needed to get to the man of God. (For us, getting to the man of God would mean getting to God!) But here's what she didn't do: She didn't crash and burn. She didn't say, "I should never have trusted God. I knew something terrible would happen."

When we lost our first baby granddaughter, Abigail Jean, at birth, my heart broke into a thousand pieces. I hurt for my daughter who held her little daughter for only a few hours. I clearly remember asking the Lord, "Why would You do that?" It was during that time I learned to stop asking the Lord why, but instead ask the Lord, "What are You going for here?" That question helps me to see a different perspective. For me, asking why to things I wouldn't understand even He if he told me puts my emotions in the driver's seat. And they would drive me to a dark place. Asking, "What are You going for?" helps me position my focus on the Lord's purposes in the situation rather than focus on how I feel and what I see. God is always working in ways we cannot see.

This woman from the Bible had experienced an unexpected, tragic loss. She went straight to the source for her need. She was hurting, yet …

6. **She was *persistent*.** She was determined. I love verse 24! "She saddled the donkey and said to her servant, 'Lead on; don't slow down for me unless I tell you.'" Picture it, bouncing around on a donkey, holding on for dear life all the while saying, "Don't slow down on my account!" She wanted to get

there as fast as she could, and her own discomfort was not an issue. Her faith had to make a journey! The same is true for us.

Like her, we must persist in faith with determination even when hope seems lost. She did not settle for anything less than God's intervention, and neither should we.

She had almost arrived at Elisha's place when he noticed her coming. He sent Gehazi to ask her if everything was okay. AGAIN, she said everything was alright. She kept right on going until she reached the man of God and explained what happened.

Elisha sent his servant to her house to lay his staff on her son's face. But she wasn't having it. Verse 30 says, "'As surely as the LORD lives and as you live, I will not leave you.' So he got up and followed her."

The Bible records that when Elisha arrived, indeed the boy was dead. He laid down on him, mouth to mouth, eyes to eyes, and hands to hands. As he stretched himself out on him, the boy's body grew warm. Elisha turned away and walked back and forth in the room and then got on the bed and stretched out on him once more. The boy sneezed seven times and opened his eyes. He called his mom in and gave him to her.

What jumps out to you about what just happened? The first thing I noticed was his healing was not immediate—it was a process. And don't miss the fact that the mother was not part of this particular process. Her part of this ended when she got to the man of God and brought him back. She was outside in the hallway! Doorways and hallways—a lot can happen there!

7. **She *surrendered* to the process.** God didn't work in an instant; He worked through a process. And she never gave up. She didn't quit! She didn't talk the problem; she talked the solution.

The Shunammite woman's heartfelt hospitality to Elisha and **simple, sincere faith** led to an amazing **series of events**. Elisha was certainly blessed. And God abundantly blessed the woman's life. Still today, God often uses His people's humble acts of service to bless both the giver and the receiver. She handled the series of events with reverence, hope, and gratitude. She kept a level of expectation of what God would do.

Now, for the rest of the story (with God, there is always more to our story). You have to see this crazy connection: Flip over to 2 Kings 8 and read verses 1–6. This happened years later.

I wish we had the space to go into detail on this as well, but part of the purpose of this resource is to help you dig into God's Word for yourself.

List your observations and lessons you can learn when the Shunammite woman told the king what happened regarding her son and the miracle God gave her.

I cannot resist sharing with you the main lesson I got from this part: She got back her land PLUS the VALUE of the crops that had been harvested. In those days, if you had to leave your home, land, and crops due to a famine or other disaster, when it was over, you could come back and ask the king for your land back.

The king not only gave her land back, but he gave her the VALUE of all the crops that could have been harvested while she was gone. Did she ask for that? No, she did not. Did she ask for a son? No, she did not. Did she expect him to die? No, she did not. Did she believe God was working through it all? Yes, she did. She made the decision in the doorway to trust God!

Focus Verse

"'Call her.' So he called her, and she stood in the doorway" (2 Kings 4:15).

Connecting the Dots

Write in your own words the connection between 2 Kings 8 and 2 Kings 4. Then write how this can help you with your decision making.

_____

_____

_____

_____

_____

Make It Personal

Now that you have read the story:

What stands out to you?

_____

_____

_____

What interesting facts did you notice in the story?

_____

_____

_____

What part of this story was meaningful to you?

_____

_____

_____

You may be standing in the doorway of decision making in hard circumstances as you are reading this. Does the story of the Shunammite woman give you hope and a process for moving forward? What would your list look like? Write the process you will take to decide how to proceed in your difficult situation.

_____

_____

_____

_____

Look again at the character list of this woman. Which one stands out to you the most and how can you apply it to your life and situations? Are there changes you need to make to become more responsive to the Lord?

_____

_____

_____

_____

SUMMARY

The Shunammite woman:

- Discerned
- Served
- Made room
- Was content
- Focused
- Was persistent
- Surrendered

Let this be the song of your heart: *"All to Jesus, I surrender, I surrender all."*

Chapter Six

There's a Boy Who Stole My Heart

"The younger son told his father,
'I want my share of your estate now before you die.'
So his father agreed to divide his wealth between his sons.
A few days later this younger son packed all his belongings and moved to a distant land,
and there he wasted all his money in wild living."
Luke 15:12–13 (NLT)

There's a boy who stole my heart—he calls me Mom.

The Lord has led me to share a very personal story, a word of encouragement, and practical application of God's Word. Today's lesson is from the story of the prodigal son and from my life.

I am the mom of a former prodigal, Jarrad. We have had several tragic events happen in our family, but loving and parenting a prodigal has been the most painful experience I have ever lived through. As stated in a previous chapter, I have buried my mom, dad, grandparents, in-laws, and granddaughter. I have also grieved over great loss in relationships and family. But nothing compared to the pain of loving and trying desperately to save a prodigal. If you love one, you know exactly what I am talking about.

Our prodigal journey was roughly twenty years long. It took Jarrad to prison for ten and a half years, from the ages of nineteen to thirty. And it took me to a place of captivity as well.

I can honestly say I have finally come to the place where I genuinely thank the Lord for this season of our lives. After much crying, complaining, begging, and generally pitching hard-headed fits, the Lord finally broke me of my unwillingness to yield to His plan and my determination to fix this. I broke because I was unwilling to bend. Don't let that happen to you. And let me tell you how the Lord brought me to the place of understanding, thanksgiving, and gratitude.

> *"You will be sorrowful, but your sorrow will turn into joy" (John 16:20 ESV).*

I have served on a church staff as director of women's ministry and as a women's minister for thirty-three years, including ten years at Prestonwood Baptist Church in Plano, Texas. I now serve as the women's minister at Green Acres Baptist Church in Tyler, Texas. I say that so you will know I love serving the Lord and I love church. My husband, John Mark, and I raised Jarrad and Haley in church from birth and we loved everything about it. But that did not exclude us (as I thought it should) from the assignment the Lord appointed to us—to parent a prodigal.

His name is Jarrad, and he was an absolute joy to parent as a child. He is tenderhearted, compassionate, always willing to give and help others. At age thirteen, a series of circumstances created "the perfect storm" in his life, including the unexpected death of his grandfather, affectionately known as "Pappaw." That pain began his journey toward full-blown rebellion and self-medication, which I will not go into, because that is his story to tell. But I CAN tell you the journey it led me on. (And may I be so honest as to say, I went into it kicking, screaming, whining, and complaining!)

My first word of encouragement is: Don't waste your time (and God's time) doing that! Once I finally got my mind and heart right with the Lord about it and accepted that this IS the assignment the Lord has chosen for me, I went ALL IN! I made up my mind (because I am a little hardheaded) to be the best mom of a prodigal that ever walked the face of the earth! I fought fearlessly for my son, because I love him passionately and I believe the Lord completely. (A lot of the story I share as "I," but please know this represents a partnership with John Mark, his dad. We handled this tragedy in different ways, but together!)

That fight was mostly done in prayer but included personal Bible study about parenting a prodigal and the close support of a group of a few faithful friends in the fight, who talked me off a cliff on more than one occasion. Let me encourage you—do not suffer in silence. I discovered this journey was more about what God wanted to do in me than in my son. I also sadly discovered that in my own way, I too was a prodigal. But that is another story!

When Jarrad was a little boy, his T-ball number was 17 and that number stuck with him even to this day. He acquired the nickname "J-Stu 17." He loved the number 17. On all his birthday cakes he wanted a "17" instead of his age; it was rather strange. Jarrad was born five weeks before my mom lost a battle with cancer at age forty. Her birthday was September 17; it just makes you wonder.

During a particularly difficult time with "J-Stu 17," I was out browsing garage sales with my husband to get my mind off things when I came across a big baseball jersey with the number 17, which I instantly connected with, and on the back in big red

Call it so, when it is not so, until it is so.

letters it read "WILDCAT." (I thought, "He's my wildcat, alright.") Something about it made me feel close to Jarrad so I wore it for the rest of the day.

Later that night as I was weeping and praying for my "wildcat," I slipped out of bed, put that jersey back on, and knelt by his bed, even though I had no idea where he was. I spent time interceding for my "Wildcat-17."

The next morning during my Bible study time, I read *Streams in the Desert*, which had this verse in Romans from the KJV Bible at the top: "God … calleth those things which be not as though they were." I love that verse, which is saying, "Call it so, when it is not so, until it is so." I knew the Lord was asking me to do that for Jarrad. I quickly looked for the reference and it took my breath away when I saw it was 4:17! I knew the Lord was speaking to me about Jarrad! How sweet and very personal of the Lord to say to me that morning, "This is FOR (4) your 17!"

Since then, the Lord has given me many more verses to encourage me with the reference 2:17 (to Jarrad) and 4:17 (for Jarrad). Let me give you a few that I hope will encourage you as well.

- "The LORD has done what he purposed" (Lam. 2:17 ESV).
- "For this light momentary affliction is preparing for us eternal weight of glory beyond all comparison" (2 Cor. 4:17 ESV).
- "But blessed is the one who trusts in the LORD, whose confidence is in him" (Jer. 17:7).
- In Matthew 17, a boy is healed!
- "Pay attention to the ministry you have received in the Lord, so that you can accomplish it" (Col. 4:17 CSB).
- "God gave these four young men an unusual aptitude for understanding every aspect of literature and wisdom" (Dan. 1:17 NLT).
- Another Bible version says, "… knowledge and skill in both books and life" (Dan. 1:17 MSG). (This is a Scripture I constantly pray for Jarrad.)

At one of my lowest and darkest points in this journey I was given a book by my dear friend, and I instantly knew and felt it was a message of promise for my number 17. It is entitled *What God Did with a Mess Like Me: 17 Truths to a Changed Life* by Jon Lineberger.

Precious one, don't allow pain, sorrow, shame, and regret to keep you at a distance from the one who loves you most. I know it hurts because we know He could change things instantly … but when He doesn't, you must continue to live in it. His divine intervention is in play whether we see it or not.

Do you have a promise for your prodigal? If not, ask the Lord for one. Mine is Isaiah 57:18 (NLT): "I have seen what they do, but I will heal them anyway! I will lead them. I will comfort those whose mourn." The Lord has indeed comforted me through this journey. And He will do the same for you if you take time to meet with Him. "Oh, turn to me, and have mercy on me! Give Your strength to Your servant, and save the son of Your maidservant" (Ps. 86:16 NKJV).

> **Precious one, don't allow pain, sorrow, shame, and regret to keep you at a distance from the one who loves you most.**

We know we can't fix or change a prodigal. Seriously, if it could have been done, I would have successfully accomplished it! But the truth is we cannot make another person walk with the Lord. We can make JUST ONE person do it and that is ourselves.

So, what CAN you do? Here are some important things we implemented that were helpful to us:

1. **PRAYER**: Meet with the Lord every day and consult Him on the matter. I learned to pray Scripture instead of spending my time "second-guessing" God's purpose, "ignorantly confusing the issue," and muddying the water," according to Job 42:1–4 in *The Message* Bible. I stopped the "what if" questions and started with "what next?" Pray for divine intervention at all costs. Pray for a spiritual awakening. It was helpful for me to fast on the seventeenth day of every month to spend extended time in prayer for Jarrad.

2. **PREPARATION**: Get in God's Word. There you will find help, comfort, strength, direction, and revelation to face the self-destructive behavior of the one you love. Start with Luke

15, the story of the prodigal. Please pay careful attention to verses 16–17 which describe the prodigal in the pig pen—sad, hungry, and in need. The Bible says, "But no one gave him anything" (Luke 15:16). Verse 17 says, "He came to his senses." For me, the Lord clearly indicated that those two things were connected. From the Lord's direction we stopped the flow of money, second chances, phone calls to get him out of trouble, and all the enabling things parents do to "help" their kid. And Jarrad had to experience the full brunt of the consequences of his choices, which landed him in jail … and he came to his senses.

3. **PURPOSE**: This is not a reflection of you as a parent. This is not a waste of time or useless. It's beneficial to the ultimate plan of God. There is a plan in play—don't forfeit your win because things have not turned out the way you planned. I remember one morning grieving deeply over yet more destructive choices Jarrad was making. There seemed to be no stopping of his downward spiral. I said to the Lord, "I hate the way he is turning out." I felt great disapproval from the Lord as He said in my heart, "He hasn't turned out yet!" The Lord tells us in Ezekiel 14:23 (KJV), "And ye shall know that I have not done without cause all that I have done in it, saith the Lord God."

4. **PERSEVERANCE:** Don't you dare quit! Love your prodigal but stop enabling them and set healthy boundaries. Start thanking the Lord for what He is doing, whether you can see it or not. Be grateful for restoration and redemption, which are two of God's finest qualities. Stop any negative thinking and pray for your homecoming and know that what the enemy intended for evil, God meant for good (see Genesis 50:20). Be brave and very courageous. I am named for Deborah in the Bible and Judges 5:21 (NLT) gives me this challenge: "March on with courage, my soul!"

In Frances Robert's devotional book, *Come Away My Beloved,* she says:

The Lord is not only mighty to save from sin, but He is mighty to save from despair, from sorrow, from disappointment, from regret, from remorse, from self-doubt, and from the hot, blinding tears of rebellion against your fateful circumstances.[6]

And let me give you one more "P" word, please—PROVIDENCE! I want to share the definition from an 1828 dictionary, not from Webster. The definition is: "God's divine call, control, and guidance over life, situations, and circumstances; making you ready for future events."

You MUST pray for providence. It helps us relinquish control over something we cannot control. And our heart can settle down during sorrow.

One verse that became my "Help me sleep at night verse" was Hosea 2:15 (NLT): "I will … transform the Valley of Trouble into a gateway of hope."

Just as the Shunammite woman from the last chapter stood in the doorway of her trouble with hope and faith, we can too. Start thanking the Lord for your hope, your homecoming, and your upcoming harvest!

Helpful resources for parenting a prodigal:

- Luke 15
- *Praying for Your Prodigal* by Kristen Sauder
- "Prayers for Your Prodigal," a prayer card from Pray Ministry
- *The Hope of a Homecoming* by Brendan O'Rourke and DeEtte Sauer
- *Prodigals and Those Who Love Them* by Ruth Bell Graham
- John Piper has written numerous articles on prodigals.
- *Setting Boundaries with Your Adult Children* by Allison Bottke
- Allison also offers a support group network called SANITY.
- *Warfare Parenting: A Daily Battle Plan to Fight for Your Child* by Laine Lawson Craft

---

6   Frances Roberts, *Come Away My Beloved* (The King's Press, 1964).

Focus Verse

"The younger son told his father, 'I want my share of your estate now before you die.' So his father agreed to divide his wealth between his sons. A few days later this younger son packed all his belongings and moved to a distant land, and there he wasted all his money in wild living" (Luke 15:12–13 NLT).

Connecting the Dots

"And I will restore to you the years that the locust hath eaten, the cankerworm, and the caterpillar, and the palmerworm, my great army which I sent among you" (Joel 2:25 KJV).

"You shall be above only, and not be beneath" (Deut. 28:13 NKJV).

"The LORD will make you the head and not the tail; you will only move upward and never downward if you listen to the LORD your God's commands I am giving you today and are careful to follow them" (Deut. 28:13 CSB).

Make It Personal

Rewrite Psalm 112:1–7 in your own words. Are you living by these principles?

_____

_____

_____

_____

_____

_____

Have you come to the point of surrendering your loved one to the Lord?

_____

_____

Have you committed to being the best mom of a prodigal that ever lived?

_____

_____

How does suffering and sorrow refine our faith?

_____

_____

_____

_____

Are you allowing this to take place in your times of pain and grief?

_____

_____

_____

_____

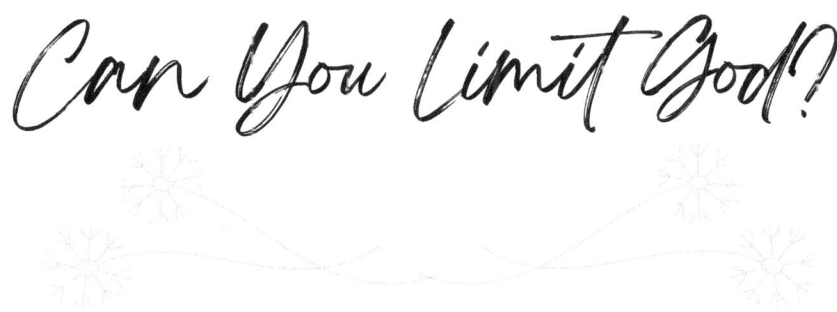

Chapter Seven

Can You Limit God?

"Yes, again and again they tempted God,
And limited the Holy One of Israel."
Psalm 78:41 (NKJV)

As I think and dream about future things, this question keeps coming up, and it has a significant impact on my way of thinking.

Can you limit God? Maybe you are like me and think obviously not, based on Psalm 78:41. We think we do not have the ability to limit God. Immediately I call to mind all the Scriptures along with Psalm 78:41 that support this belief.

The Bible says in:

- Genesis 18:14 (NKJV): "Is anything too hard for the LORD?"
- Matthew 19:26: "With God all things are possible."
- Luke 18:27 (NASB): "The things that are impossible with people are possible with God."
- 2 Chronicles 16:9 (NLT): "The eyes of the LORD search the whole earth in order to strengthen those whose hearts are fully committed to him."

Therefore, we know God is ABLE! He is sovereign. He is in control of everything, everywhere, all the time. He is willing, longing, and looking to do great things in our life. His Word tell us He has no limits, no boundaries, no restrictions. No one can stop Him! He is limitless. That is TRUTH!

So, is the answer, no, we cannot limit God?

That's what I thought for years. Nobody can stop God. He's going to do whatever He wants to do. I don't have any ability to stop Him or His work. Or do I?

Read Psalm 78:41 (NLT): "Again and again, they tested God's patience and provoked the Holy One of Israel."

If you know me, you've heard me say MANY times, "You can't just jerk a verse." I don't like taking one verse out of a passage. We must keep it in context. So, let's back up to understand God's previous message.

Basically, in Psalm 78, the Lord commands His people to listen to His teaching and open their ears to what He is saying. He says He will teach us hidden lessons and stories that our ancestors handed down. He tells us not to hide these truths from our children, but to tell the next generation about the glorious deeds of the Lord, and to tell of His might and power and the miracles He did. "So each generation should set its hope anew on God" (Ps. 78:7 NLT). (I love that part!) He said He does not want us to be like our ancestors, "stubborn, rebellious, and unfaithful, refusing to give their hearts to God" (Ps. 78:8 NLT). However, we are exactly like our ancestors—actually, worse. We have disobeyed God's Word. We have been unwilling to repent and continued in our stubborn, rebellious ways.

And that's the reason for verse 41.

> *"Yes, again and again they tempted God, and limited the Holy One of Israel" (Ps. 78:41 NKJV).*

Now, what is the answer to the question: Can we limit God?

YES! Yes, we can limit God. We can limit His power at work in our life. We can forfeit His activity. And frankly, that scares me, and I wish it wasn't true.

Psalm 78:41 is recorded for our benefit and our warning. I researched this Scripture and prayed for weeks for God to give me spiritual insight and understanding into this. I knew God was trying to say something to me through this verse. Please know that I am not a theologian. I do not have extensive seminary education in Greek and Hebrew. But I will tell you what I do have. I have the Holy Spirit in my heart to enlighten Scripture to me so I may understand it and apply it. The Bible says not to be hearers only of God's Word, but to be what? Doers. (See James 1:22.) Being a "doer" of God's Word means we put it into our lives. We practice it.

> "Give me understanding [a teachable heart and the ability to learn], that I may keep Your law; and observe it with all my heart" (Ps. 119:34 AMP).

That means practice it!

> "So pay attention to how you hear. To those who listen to my teaching, more understanding will be given. But for those who are not listening, even what they think they understand will be taken away from them" (Luke 8:18 NLT).

What's helpful to me in understanding Scripture is to look up the original meaning of the words (in Greek and Hebrew). I do that through a helpful website: blueletterbible.org. Along with that I look up the Scripture in various Bible translations. I also use other dictionaries to define words along with looking up synonyms and antonyms of each word. So, with this Scripture I pulled together about five translations and came up with a list of what the people did: They rebelled, grieved, tested, and provoked. They frustrated, tempted, forgot, and vexed (I like that word, vexed—it means irritated or difficult). The people limited the Holy One of Israel by their behavior. Let that settle in for a minute. God wanted to do some things that He would not do. God could have done things for them but chose not to because of what they did.

I wonder what the Lord would say about me—about us—today? Would my attitudes and actions be reflected on this list of behaviors?

Now, let's tease this out (as we say in the South) for deeper understanding.

The Word tells us in Psalm 78:42 (NLT): "They did not remember his power and how he rescued them from their enemies." In other words, they did not acknowledge, appreciate, or think about what the Lord had done for them.

I tell my grandkids: "No gratitude leads to a bad attitude."

Read verse 56: "But they kept testing and rebelling against God Most High. They did not obey his laws." Although God did all this for them, they continued to test His patience.

The passage says "again and again" they responded the same way. Over and over—no change, no self-correcting, no realigning, no adjustments, no apologies to the Lord—the same rebellious behavior and ungrateful attitude.

Self-evaluation: How do YOU respond AGAIN and AGAIN?

No gratitude leads to a bad attitude.

My grandkids were at my house a few weeks ago and my oldest, Clark, is so tender-hearted. He is just wired in the sweetest way. We were playing outside on the patio, and in our garage we have a big jar full of change. Clark came to the patio table where I was sitting and put down a quarter. I could tell he was about to cry. He said, "Dodie, I took a quarter from your jar. I'm sorry! I will not do that again." Now I was crying.

He didn't do what was right and it bothered him. But he corrected it. He wanted to make it right. And I loved it. He self-corrected. I didn't catch him and make him do what was right. I would never have known if he had not told me. He self-reported.

I thanked him and let him know how great that made me feel and how proud I was of him. We talked about integrity, actions, and how we honor God by doing right. (In my mind, I was thinking, *Buddy, you are at Dodie's house. You don't have to self-report.*)

Guess what I did next. I told him, "Now you walk over to that big jar of change and get yourself a handful of quarters!" I wanted to bless his actions. His wrong behavior would have landed him one quarter. But his repentance landed him about twenty quarters.

In a way, that's what the Lord does with us. When we seek forgiveness instead of being forgetful and self-deserving, the Lord says He will bless our obedience.

Personal application: Is there any area of your life where you need to self-correct?

So, here's the thing that really bothered me about the text. The problem was with God's people, not the world. From this passage, He tells us that His limitations are not coming from the world—they are coming from His own people. People who say they love Him and say they will follow Him. It's not people outside the church that are the problem here; it's people inside the church that are limiting God. Oh, wow! So, what do we do to prevent limiting God?

> **Is there any area of your life where you need to self-correct?**

> *"If My people [not all people] who are called by My name will humble themselves, and pray and seek My face, and turn from their wicked ways, then I will hear from heaven, and will forgive their sin and heal their land" (2 Chron. 7:14 NKJV, insert mine).*

Revival starts from within the church—with God's people. And now we know that we can hinder it!

We can limit His movement, His purposes, His intentions, and His plans by our sin of turning from His Word in disobedience. And in doing so we limit His activity in our lives and our usefulness to Him. Worse yet, it perpetuates to the next generation. The enemy of your soul (the devil) seeks to render us helpless, useless, and unproductive in the things of God.

"The thief comes only to steal and kill and destroy; I have come that they may have life, and have it to the full" (John 10:10).

I've been thinking about the various ways I have been limiting God. I never intended to do that, and I don't desire to do that, but the truth is, according to my actions, I do limit God. One thing I have learned through this growth process is instead of praying, "Lord, send revival, send revival," I should start removing the obstacles I have put in the way of revival.

What does God say about obstacles in the Psalm passage alone, and what limits Him?

1. **Our disobedience**: Spiritual indifference, apathy, laziness, personal preferences, stubbornness, and unwillingness to follow God (which is really a lack of desire to know Him).
2. **Our unbelief**: All the miracles He displayed in front of their very eyes and yet, every difficulty, every unexpected hard thing, became an opportunity for them to whine, complain, and not believe His Word. "And he did not do many mighty works there, because of their unbelief" (Matt. 13:58 ESV).
3. **Our forgetfulness**: Our lack of appreciation, no gratitude, and no thankfulness.

And I am going to add one more that I truly believe the Lord pointed out to me from this list. My mom used to say this word a lot: *Snarkiness!* It's being short-tempered and short-sighted, always having a low level of frustration and irritability.

Snarkiness includes whining and complaining, comparing our lives and circumstances to others, and feeling like things are unfair. A practice that helps me identify areas in my life that need improvement is this: Take a blank sheet or paper. Draw a line from top to bottom down the middle (now you have two columns). At the top of the left-hand column, write in large letters: STOP. On the right-hand side, write: START.

Now, ask the Lord this: *Lord, is there anything in my life I need to STOP doing?*

Now for the hard part. Sit still and be quiet. Focus. Concentrate on hearing the Lord's voice in your heart and in your head. Write down everything He says. I'll never forget the first time I did this exercise. Honestly, I wrote two pages of things I needed to STOP doing!

Now, ask the Lord this: *Lord, is there anything in my life I need to START doing?*

Follow the same process. Now, DO those things and STOP doing the others! This will make you sensitive to the voice of the Lord and help you recognize the Lord at work in your life. You may not realize how you've been hindering and limiting God.

We know from these verses that limiting God is connected to the liberty of the Holy Spirit at work in our lives. We can be in one of two places. Either God has full liberty to work in your life, or we have limited God's work in our life.

> *"Now to him who is able to do immeasurably more than all we ask or imagine, according to his power that is at work within us" (Eph. 3:20).*

He is able to do it, if you do not limit Him. You have the ability to forfeit His work and frustrate His plans and purposes. But He can do more than we ask or imagine. It is according to His power at work within us. How is this power activated? By our faith and yielded heart in agreement with His power.

Here is a biblical truth: When we limit God, we grieve the Holy Spirit!

> *"And do not grieve the Holy Spirit of God, with whom you were sealed for the day of redemption" (Eph. 4:30).*

And do not bring sorrow to God's Holy Spirit by the way you live. What does it mean to grieve the Holy Spirit? I had so much fun this day of my study because you know I love definitions!

Here's the definition of grieving the Holy Spirit: When you *deliberately or inadvertently* behave in a way that is inimical (pronounced *uh-ri-muh-kl*) to your spiritual improvement.

Inimical? Who says *inimical?* But I love new words and when I looked it up, I am not even kidding … the definition of *inimical* is being obstructive, harmful, and LIMITING! It describes one who is uncooperative and unresponsive to the Lord, His Word, and His ways.

Let me crank down on one other observation since we are cranking away here. My grandma would say, "OH, now you are cooking with bacon grease!"

Go back to definition of grieving the Holy Spirit. It uses the words *deliberately or inadvertently*. It might sound something like this: "Oh, I didn't mean to," or, "I didn't intend to," or, "It wasn't on purpose. I wasn't planning to be disobedient. I didn't mean to *not* do what I said I was going to do."

Please note: The results are the same, whether intentional or not. Either way, the consequences are the same. Now you have consequences to deal with. You have set things in motion that will take you down a destructive path.

So, here's what I suggest (my self-correction). It's something I am doing in my own life.

I make decisions using God's Word and/or wise counsel about what needs to happen or what I need to do. Then I do it with intentionality and integrity.

In Psalm 78, God wanted them to remember so the next generation could set their hope anew on the Lord. What we are or are not doing today has an impact on the next generation. Think of practical, daily ways you can show gratitude to the Lord. You can tell others of His goodness, faithfulness, and generosity to you as a public reminder proclaiming His faithfulness and His goodness.

I am starting to do this on a regular basis—remembering what the Lord has done and expressing my gratitude and sharing it with others. I shared a photo in a post of my husband and a nine-pound bass … actually nine pounds three ounces (fishermen—they are so picky about size and weight). I clearly remember many days when I didn't know if he would ever fish again when his heart was failing.

Ephesians 5:17 (KJV) says, "Wherefore be ye not unwise, but understanding what the will of the Lord is." The Lord wants to reveal His will for us, but in order to receive that understanding we must remove our limits. Don't limit what you think God can do in and through you and in and through your situation.

Focus Verse

"Yes, again and again they tempted God, and limited the Holy One of Israel"
(Ps. 78:41 NKJV).

Connecting the Dots

Over and over the Bible says of the disciples that they did not know, they did not understand, or they thought Jesus was doing one thing when He was doing something different. But there are examples in God's Word of people who got it right—people who did not limit God.

Great faith was spoken of just a few people in God's Word:

1. **The Centurion Man**
   His story is found in Matthew chapter 8. "When Jesus heard this, he marveled and said to those who followed him, 'Truly I tell you, with no one is Israel have I found such faith'" (Matt. 8:10 ESV).
2. **A Gentile Woman**
   Her daughter was healed from demon possession. "Jesus said to her, 'Your faith is great. Your request is granted'" (Matt. 15:28 NLT).
3. **A Blind Man**
   "They went right into the house where he was staying, and Jesus asked them, 'Do you believe I can make you see?' 'Yes, Lord,' they told him, 'we do.' Then he touched their eyes and

said, 'Because of your faith, it will happen'" (Matt. 9:28–29 NLT).

4. **A Woman with a Long-Term Issue**
   "Jesus turned around, and when he saw her he said, 'Daughter, be encouraged! Your faith has made you well.' And the woman was healed at that moment" (Matt. 9:22 NLT).

In these verses, "Your faith" wasn't said of John the Baptist. It wasn't said of the disciples. Who was it said of? The people who believed God.

God's Word doesn't say that God's miracles have made you well, or God's hand has healed you. It says that *what they did* moved God and that is what caused God to act on their behalf. They believed.

They removed all limits to what God wanted to do in their lives.

Make It Personal

Personal application: Is there any area of your life where you need to self-correct?

_____

_____

_____

Ask the Lord today: *Show me how I am limiting You.*

Spend a few minutes reading Psalm 139. Take some notes on how this chapter speaks to you and pay close attention to verses 23–24.

SUMMARY

Sin separates us from God like a wall between our heart and His Word. To demolish the wall is to confess, repent, and live according to God's Word and will for our lives so we are not limiting His work in us and through us.

Chapter Eight

March On in Courage

"I keep my eyes always on the LORD.
With him at my right hand, I will not be shaken."
Psalm 16:8
"O my soul, march on in strength!"
Judges 5:21 (NKJV)

My life was changed by one woman stepping into the life of one woman.

It was on a day when my mom was contemplating suicide that Mrs. Jean (a sweet lady from next door) came over for a visit and invited my mom to church. In church the next day my mom heard about God's love and gave her life to Christ. The women's group welcomed her with open arms. They called the group the "Deborah class." They gave her a Bible and began to pour into her life. My mom began to thrive, and her life was changed. When I was born, she named me Deborah Jean.

Because of that love and influence she did not raise her children the way she was raised and became our family's first-generation Christian. Research indicates and statistics can prove that the negative things that happened to my mom growing up would also happen to me and be repeated in cycles for generations. However, research failed to factor in the redemptive power of Jesus Christ at work in the life of one woman!

Then there was me. As a grieving young woman with a five-week-old baby boy, I found myself at a dark place in life. Then one woman stepped into *my* life. She spoke truth into my life and taught me how to walk with the Lord and how pain can be used for progress. She championed my faith! She recognized and affirmed God's call on my life to ministry, and she frankly insisted on my spiritual growth. So many times, I wanted to quit but she would have none of that, not on her watch!

Here comes that lump again.

Now, you don't know me, but I have had the greatest privilege of leading women's ministry for thirty-three years—ten years at one of the largest churches in the United States. You need to know it was not because of skill, education, or any other personal ability. I have committed my life to ministry because years ago one woman became involved in the life of one woman, and it changed the course of history.

Proverbs 31:26 (NLT): "When she speaks, her words are wise, and she gives instructions with kindness."

Since then, many women have stepped into the lives of many women and one by one lives have been changed, history has been altered, and the gates of hell have been pushed back.

My prayer for this lesson is Proverbs 31:26 (NLT): "When she speaks, her words are wise, and she gives instructions with kindness."

Let's look into the lives of a few girls in history that God tested and the enemy sifted, yet they preserved, remained faithful, and were not shaken. Their stories are told in God's Word and hold valuable life lessons for us as we seek to do the same.

Girl #1—my namesake, Deborah. Her story is found in Judges chapter 4. It would be so helpful if you could read her story in your Bible and make some personal notes for yourself. Plus, you might not believe it if you don't see what happens with your own eyes, because Girl #2 also shows up in this story … with a tent peg!

But before we get to the fun of that, let's take a look at the story and see what we can learn and apply to our lives. Please meet me on the pages of Judges 4. Here's the back story to catch us up in the storyline:

- Barak and Deborah (a judge) are fighting Sisera (the commander of Jabin's army—the enemy!).
- Barak told Deborah he wanted her by his side in this fight, and she was willing to fight!
- The Lord had promised victory but said it would be at the hands of a woman (and everyone assumed that would be Deborah—but press pause on that!).
- In this intense battle the Bible says that ALL of Sisera's warriors were killed. However, Sisera escaped.

A few things to note about Deborah:

- She was known for her relationship with God and had a good reputation for bravery.
- She was trustworthy, wise, and displayed great courage.
- She believed God would bring victory in her battles. She fought hard and had grit!
- She helped others fulfill their God-given assignments.
- She modeled a posture of humility and worship, reminding us to celebrate God's work.

Now, let's read verse 17. Enter stage left, Girl #2—Jael.

- Sisera ran into Jael's tent. And it is interesting to know why—the Bible says because their families had been friends. Hmm … the enemy thinks he has access to "my tent" and my family because of how he has worked in prior generations. But NOT ON MY WATCH!
- Sisera asked her to hide him, so she did, under a blanket. Oh, she's smart!
- The Bible says she offered him something warm to drink (milk and brownies, I'm sure).
- So he fell asleep. And the Bible says Jael crept up with a hammer and drove a tent peg through his temple and he died.

- And victory was indeed given through the hands of a woman that day but not the one on the frontlines. It was the one who worked behind the scenes and stopped the enemy dead in his tracks.

A few things to note about Jael:

- She is somewhat unknown. She was not a soldier nor a prophet nor a judge. She was a tent-dwelling woman. But she was a woman who used the intuition and ability the Lord had given her, and it changed the course of history.
- She displayed courage and strength. I'm just saying'—it was a tent peg through the temple!
- She was alert and paid attention to God's promptings.
- She used what she had, and she did what she could. "She has done what she could."

You don't have to be on center stage to make a great impact. Though Jael played a brief role, her actions were pivotal in Israel's victory.

Crazy story but a game changer!

Obviously, we don't live in tents, but the devil can get in our house, and in your head space—your thoughts, your attitudes, your words, and your actions. And if he has somehow made it into your tent because of past family junk, go ahead and grab a tent peg. God's Word is like a tent peg to get the devil out of your house.

> *"For among them are those who creep into households and capture weak women, burdened with sins and led astray by various passions"* (2 Tim. 3:6 ESV).

Devil might "oughta" think twice before he plays games with a courageous woman of God! Or he's going to have one heck of a headache! The Lord is still looking for women today that will step up and lead the fight and use the abilities the Lord has given them to bring victory.

> *"The eyes of the LORD search the whole earth in order to strengthen those whose hearts are fully committed to him"* (2 Chron. 16:9 NLT).

Acts 20:24 (NLT) reminds us: "But my life is worth nothing to me unless I use it for finishing the work assigned me by the Lord Jesus."

The Lord gave a BIG VICTORY that day—through the hand of a woman!

Judges chapter 5 goes on to tell of the great praise and worship celebration that followed: "March on, my soul, in strength!" (Judg 5:21 CSB).

Say it with me: "MARCH ON, my soul, in strength!" You can be confident that the Lord has gone before you!

Girl #3—her name is not given (perhaps so we could all relate to her). Her story is in Matthew chapter 9, and it's about a woman who came to Jesus. The Bible said she had a devastating problem, an issue she could not resolve although she had tried everything. But then in verse 21, the Bible records something that will be extremely helpful to us. God's Word says, "She said to herself, 'If I only touch his cloak, I will be healed.'" Take note that she said it to herself—nobody said it to her.

You are seen! Jesus sees YOU!

Caution—be careful about what our mind and thoughts say, as well as what narratives we play. Be careful what voices we listen to, with our own sometimes being the worst. Verse 22 records the sweetest thing that changed her life: "Jesus turned and saw her."

You are seen! Jesus sees YOU! And He cares about every detail of your life and circumstances.

> *The LORD directs the steps of the godly. He delights in every detail of their lives. Though they stumble, they will never fall, for the LORD holds them by the hand. Once I was young, and now I am old. Yet I have never seen the godly abandoned or their children begging for bread. (Psalm 37:23–25 NLT)*

"Jesus turned around, and when he saw her, he said, 'Daughter, be encouraged! Your faith has made you well.' And the woman was healed at that moment" (Matt. 9:22 NLT).

These women are what I call "courageously faithful"! And I want to be that as well! They persevered through unexpected circumstances, painful challenges, uncertainty, insecurity, frustration, tears, and much more.

I once had a terrible year with plantar fasciitis, a hairline fracture, and arthritis in my left foot.

I had pain on some level every single day. It was so frustrating. When I got out of bed and that foot hit the floor, there was pain.

I did all the things. I walked in a boot for weeks, slept in a brace every night, got shots, did all manner of crazy exercises, and massaged it every morning and every night to get the swelling down. One morning I got up and put my foot down and noticed it wasn't as painful as usual. I began to massage it and noticed it was not as swollen as usual. As I was sitting there thinking about the little progress that had been made, I heard the Lord say, "I CREATED YOU TO HEAL!" He has created our bodies, our minds, and our hearts to heal. We must be sure we are working the healing process. Meeting with the Healer on a daily basis is paramount to our healing.

EVEN THOUGH! Two words that change everything!

Girl #4 is not named in God's Word. She is mentioned in Judges 13. We know her as Sampson's mom. I had heard all about Sampson, but I didn't know about his mom. She was the wife of Manoah, and the Bible says in Judges 13:3 (NLT), "Even though you have been unable to have children, you will soon become pregnant and give birth to a son." Another translation says, "You are barren and childless" (NIV).

That seems harsh…. It sounds like, "You don't have any children, and you never will."

EVEN THOUGH! Two words that change everything! And you know how I love definitions. So, do you know what *even though* means? It means "despite the facts." Despite. The. Facts. Now, think about that for a moment.

Do you know what—more than anything else—has gotten me off track with the Lord, gotten me stuck in a pit, thinking devastating thoughts and destructive attitudes, and unable (probably more like unwilling) to move forward in faith?

Can I share with you what has been the most heartbreaking thing to me in life? **The facts**! It's the stinkin' facts!

It's sitting in meetings where someone gives you the facts.

Or sitting alone realizing what the facts of the matter are.

- The fact is your mom has aggressive cancer and without a miracle it will be fatal.
- The fact is your dad is dying from alcoholism and won't stop drinking.
- The fact is your son has a life-threatening addiction.
- The fact is your son has been sentenced to ten and a half years in prison.
- The fact is your daughter must give birth to a baby that will not live.
- The fact is your husband needs a heart transplant. And he will die if he doesn't get a new heart very soon.

Does anybody relate to the overwhelming, heartbreaking facts of life?

But we cannot live in fear of the facts! We can't stay stuck in the facts! We can't be wimpy and whiny because we don't like the facts. I am not saying ignore the facts. I'm saying that the Lord knows the facts, He allowed the facts, and He says, "EVEN THOUGH …"! (Despite the facts!)

I guess that's what I love so much about "EVEN THOUGH"!

Despite the facts, it doesn't matter what the facts are. GOD is in control of THIS situation!

Say that with me: "Even though … !" What facts are you dealing with right now?

> *Even though the fig trees have no blossoms, and there are no grapes on the vines; even though the olive crop fails, and the fields lie empty and barren; even though the flocks die in the fields, and the cattle barns are empty, yet I will rejoice in the Lord! I will be joyful in the God of my salvation! The Sovereign Lord is my strength! He makes me as surefooted as a deer, able to tread upon the heights. (Habakkuk 3:17–19 NLT)*

Biblical principle: God puts you in a particular place for a specific reason to accomplish an important thing—*despite the facts.*

We must be faithful in our place. Embrace our place. Stop whining, complaining, and comparing.

March on—move forward, oh my soul, in courage.

December 2023 was a terrible and hard month for me and my family. I feared losing someone I love very much. Circumstances scared me. It grieved me terribly. It was sad. And there was nothing I could do but pray and try to remain hopeful. It consumed my thoughts. And every call to them that went to voicemail convinced me that I would never see them again. One day I wasn't doing such a great job at being hopeful. (I might have been whining and complaining—I cannot confirm nor deny my attitude that day.) But I can confirm for you what God said to me, and I didn't think it wasn't very nice!

This is what I heard from the Lord: "Get off it … right now!"

Maybe that's for someone today: "Get off it … right now!"

I was so exhausted from worry and overwhelmed with "what if" that I could not think straight. I could not sleep, and I did not have an appetite. Celebrating Christmas was difficult. In other words, I let the fear of loss take me to a very unhealthy place.

But I heard the Lord loud and clear: "Get off it! And get on with it!"

If you want to make the devil mad, get happy! Take back what he has stolen from you!

CHOOSE JOY! And march on!

The enemy doesn't fight us because we are weak. The enemy fights us because we are becoming strong.

He wants us to stay weak.

We can feel sorrow and yet still celebrate the goodness of God.

Focus Verses

"I keep my eyes always on the LORD. With him at my right hand, I will not be shaken" (Ps. 16:8).

"O my soul, march on in strength!" (Judg. 5:21 NKJV).

Another life-changing verse for me: "And it is a good thing to receive wealth from God and the good health to enjoy it. To enjoy your work and accept your lot in life—this is indeed a gift from God" (Eccles. 5:19 NLT).

Connecting the Dots

Oh, darlin', we get so messed up because we can't/wont/don't accept our lot in life. That means our assignment from God. I didn't want to parent a prodigal and then parent a prisoner. I didn't want to bury my mom when she was forty. I didn't want to bury a baby granddaughter. I hated spending Mother's Day weekend in a prison visitation room, along with a decade of Christmases.

BUT this was my lot in life. It was assigned or allowed by God. It was given to me for my benefit, the benefit of others, and for the glory of God as He pruned me to be the women He created me to be.

The passage goes on to say, "This is a gift of God. They seldom reflect on the days of their life, because God keeps them occupied with gladness of heart"(Eccles. 5:19–20 NIV). That means they don't keep looking back with shame or regret. They don't waste time asking, "WHY? WHEN?" And my favorite part: God keeps them occupied with gladness or joy of heart.

With our eyes on the Lord, we will not be shaken, and we are able to march on in courage.

Make It Personal

What has you occupied right now? What is consuming your thoughts?

_____

_____

_____

_____

_____

_____

What are you focused on and fixated about? The Bible says in Psalm 34:18 (CSB), "The Lord is near the brokenhearted; he saves those crushed in spirit."

_____

_____

_____

_____

SUMMARY

I hope you feel the presence of the Lord today and that you are spending time on the pages of His Word. He will meet you there for sure! He will comfort you and direct your steps and decisions.

> *Trust GOD from the bottom of your heart; don't try to figure out everything on your own. Listen for GOD's voice in everything you do, everywhere you go; he's the one who will keep you on track. Don't assume that you know it all. Run to GOD! Run from evil! Your body will glow with health, your very bones will vibrate with life! Honor GOD with everything you own; give him the first and the best. Your barns will burst, your wine vats will brim over. But don't, dear friend, resent GOD's discipline; don't sulk under his loving correction. It's the child he loves that GOD corrects; a father's delight is behind all this. (Proverbs 3:6–12 MSG)*

You can carry sorrow and celebration at the same time!

He promises you riches stored in secret places!

Here I've paraphrased Isaiah 45:1–3:

> *God will give you a great anointing for the assignment.*

> *He will empower your hands for the task.*

> *He will open doors, level mountains, smash gates, cut through iron.*

> *He will go before you and make the crooked places straight.*

> *He will give you treasures hidden in darkness and riches stored in secret places.*

> *So you WILL KNOW He is the One who calls YOU by name!*

Chapter Nine

The Life-Changing Power of Two Words

"Teach me to do your will, for you are my God.
May your gracious Spirit lead me forward on a firm footing."
Psalm 143:10 (NLT)

I have never been a woman of few words. (I know, you are shocked by that!) The more I walk with the Lord, the more I realize that often His words are few, His direction is clear, and He awaits our response. There are times in my life I have felt I was waiting on God to do something, change something, or help me with something. All the while He was waiting on *me* to do something or change something.

In this chapter I'd like to share a personal story of how God used two words to help me align myself with His Word, His work, His purposes, and His plan. Things were much harder than they needed to be because I did not do what God was waiting for. I was overthinking circumstances, playing out worst-case scenarios, and constantly asking myself, "What if … ?" Those two words, *what if*, along with *now what* and *I can't*, almost destroyed me.

Through God's Word, He used these two words to set my feet on a firm footing. He shifted my perspective from the *unfairness* of it all to the *unfolding* of it all.

(That's why Twenty Minutes a Day for the Rest of Your Life is so important.)

Two words:

1. So that …
2. Even if …
3. If you …

You are going to be surprised (and hopefully very blessed) at how many times God says "so that" in His Word. However, we will wait until the next chapter because the weight and explanation of it needs to stand alone. It's my favorite!

So, let's look at these two words: *Even if*.

Our family has had some "familiar struggles" cycle back into our lives. Why the Lord has allowed them again I will never know nor understand. And although I cannot trace His hand into the future, I can trace His hand of faithfulness from the past!

Psalm 27:3 (NLT)

Read all of Psalm 27 to connect with the following high points in this chapter of the Bible.

Verse 1: "The LORD is my light and my salvation—so why should I be afraid? The LORD is my fortress, protecting me from danger, so why should I tremble?"

Verse 3: "Though a mighty army surrounds me, my heart will not be afraid. **EVEN IF** I am attacked, I will remain confident" (emphasis mine).

Verse 8: "My heart has heard you say, 'Come and talk with me.' And my heart responds, 'LORD, I am coming.'"

Verse 13: "Yet I am confident I will see the LORD's goodness while I am here in the land of the living."

Verse 14: "Wait patiently for the LORD. Be brave and courageous. Yes, wait patiently for the LORD."

Fear is an overwhelming shadow of darkness that paralyzes and imprisons us. It grips our emotions and feeds our insecurity and uncertainty. And then we begin to ask ourselves, "What if … ?" But instead of asking, "What if … ?" we can conquer our fear by stepping into the light of God's Word and say, "Even if …" That is the confidence that comes from our faith and trusting God.

Psalm 119:130 says, "The unfolding of your words gives light; it gives understanding to the simple."

When going through times of sorrow, suffering, or trials, we can be confident God will see us through because of two little words: *Even if.*

Those two small words are one powerful declaration: "Even if …" They are the words of someone who has decided to trust God no matter what.

"Even if" describes something that remains true or will happen, regardless of a possible or unfavorable con-

> **"Even if" describes something that remains true or will happen, regardless of a possible or unfavorable condition.**

dition. It Indicates that a particular fact does not negate that something else is still true. It shows that your decision or belief will stay the same no matter what happens. It means CHOOSING faith and courage, perseverance and spiritual tenacity, EVEN IF you are afraid, anxious, or hurt.

- Even if they attack me, I will remain confident.
- Even if I fail, I will keep trying.
- Even if answers are delayed, I will wait patiently.
- Even if the battle rages on, I will armor up.
- Even if the healing doesn't come, I will trust the Lord.
- Even if trouble rises up, I won't be shaken.
- Even if turmoil surrounds me, I'll remain at peace.

These words say, "I still trust Him. I still worship Him. I still believe Him. And I will be part of God's plan that will ultimately bring Him glory." They are a declaration that our faith is not based on outcomes but on the unchanging character of God.

> *I will never forget this awful time, as I grieve over my loss. Yet I still dare to hope when I remember this: The faithful love of the LORD never ends! His mercies never cease. Great is his faithfulness; his mercies begin afresh each morning. I say to myself, "The LORD is my inheritance; therefore, I will hope in him!" The LORD is good to those who depend on him, to those who search for him. So, it is good to wait quietly for salvation from the LORD. (Lamentations 3:20–26 NLT)*

What have you been saying to yourself?

- "I can't handle this."
- "I can't do it anymore."
- "I am losing my mind."
- "This is so unfair."
- "This is killing me."
- "I dread this."
- "It's such a waste."
- "This is too hard."

What should you be saying to yourself?

The Lord has really been on me lately about what I am saying to myself. I am not even kidding; this is what I wrote in my Bible study journal last week … to myself!

Debbie! Listen, Debbie! You better tell yourself the TRUTH of God's Word or your present reality will be debilitating to you!

So, I say to myself: *What does God's Word say about it?*

Another thing the Lord is stirring up in me and has caused me to feel strongly about is that we need to help each other with our thoughts and words. We need to speak truth into one another's lives.

Around this same time, I was reading an article in *Psychology Today* that discussed how the direction of a person's gaze gives insight into their intentions and future decisions.

It's so true! I barely gazed over at Chick-fil-A and before I knew it, I was in the drive through (and you know once you are in that drive through, there is no turning back!). But I was planning to order a salad, until I gazed at the menu and saw the chicken sandwich meal deal … with a free cookie.

Remember the story of the woman with the issue of blood? It's in Matthew chapter 9. She said to herself, "If I can just get to Jesus, I will be healed."

Before we leave this "even if" principle, I want to point out two more stories I hope will build up your faith and give you a different mindset.

The first one is probably a familiar story to you—the story of Shadrach, Meshach, and Abednego.

But please look at it with fresh eyes and gaze on over to the "even if" statement they made. As a reminder, these three guys were ordered to bow down to a golden statue that Nebuchadnezzar worshiped. But they would not. They chose to remain faithful to the Lord. They were told they would be thrown into a fiery furnace, and this was their response:

> *If we are thrown into the blazing furnace, the God whom we serve is able to save us. He will rescue us from your power, Your Majesty. But* **EVEN IF** *he doesn't, we want to make it clear to you, Your Majesty, that we will never serve your gods or worship the gold statue you have set up.* (*Daniel 3:17–18 NLT, emphasis mine*)

And with that, they were thrown into a fiery furnace that was heated up seven times hotter than usual.

I am paraphrasing verse 25 here: Then Nebuchadnezzar said, "I see four men walking around in the fire. They aren't even hurt by the flames and the fourth looks like the Son of God."

"Even if" faith is not shaken by fiery trails and the storms of life—it is strengthened by it.

The kind of faith that says, "My God is able … and *even if* He doesn't, I'm still His and I still believe!"

Sometimes God doesn't stop you from being thrown into the furnace because He has a point to prove to the people who threw you in.

What I especially love about Shadrach, Meshach, and Abednego is that after they came through the furnace, there was no smell of fire or even smoke on them.

Child of God, you don't have to smell like what you have been through!

Our hope is not based on "What if … ?" It is anchored in "Even if …"!

And one more story of "even if" faith:

> *Even if the fig tree does not blossom, and there is no fruit on the vines, if the yield of the olive fails, and the fields produce no food, even if the flock disappears from the fold, and there are no cattle in the stalls, yet I will triumph in the LORD, I will rejoice in the God of my salvation. (Habakkuk 3:17–18 NASB)*

Even if everything around you feels empty, God is still enough. Habakkuk was experiencing loss, devastation, and emptiness, yet he made a choice to rejoice!

"Even If" by MercyMe (chorus):

> *I know You're able and I know You can*
> *Save through the fire with Your mighty hand*
> *But even if You don't*
> *My hope is You alone[7]*

The words to the song above by MercyMe are especially meaningful to me. I encourage you to look up all of the lyrics so you can see how

---

7   MercyMe, "Even If," *Lifer,* Fair Trade Services, 2017.

God uses this song to minister to us when we are going through the fire.

God puts you in a particular place for a specific reason to accomplish an important thing. Embrace your place even if trouble comes your way!

Please indulge me for one more two-word challenge: **"IF YOU ..."**

Lastly, we are going to look at a few verses (and there are many!) that God's promise or His response to us is contingent on our actions. Part is our responsibility, and the other part is His.

The promise of salvation is conditional: "If you openly declare that Jesus is Lord and believe in your heart that God raised him from the dead, you will be saved" (Rom. 10:9 NLT).

> *My son,* **IF YOU** *receive my words, and treasure my commands within you, so that you incline your ear to wisdom, and [if you] apply your heart to understanding; yes,* **IF YOU** *cry out for discernment, and [if you] lift up your voice for understanding,* **IF YOU** *seek her as silver, and [if you] search for her as for hidden treasures; then you will understand the fear of the LORD, and find the knowledge of God. (Proverbs 2:1–5 NKJV, emphasis and inserts mine)*

The promise of understanding the fear of the Lord and finding knowledge of God comes only AFTER the "IF YOU" conditions are met.

"IF YOU keep My commandments, you will abide in My love" (John 15:10 NKJV, emphasis mine).

The opposite is also true: If you are not keeping His commandments, which means obeying His Word,

you will not abide in His love—you will forfeit it.

Focus Verse

"Teach me to do your will, for you are my God. May your gracious Spirit lead me forward on a firm footing" (Ps. 143:10 NLT).

Connecting the Dots

The Holy Spirit leads us to a firm footing through God's Word, our prayers, and applying what we learn to our daily lives. He teaches us His will. "Even if … I will trust in God and believe His Word, knowing He has gone before me, and is with me through it all, no matter what."

Make It Personal

What have you been saying to yourself?

_____

_____

_____

What should you be saying to yourself?

_____

_____

_____

What changes do you need to make to step up to "even if" faith?

_____

_____

_____

What has God been asking you to do that fear has prevented you from moving forward?

_____

_____

_____

SUMMARY

Let's wrap this up with a note about Martha. John 11:40 (NKJV) says, "Jesus said to her, 'Did I not say to you that *if you* would believe you would see the glory of God?'" (emphasis mine).

She was in danger of becoming hard-hearted and spiritually blind instead of experiencing the glory of God. She would have gone back to her home unchanged and disillusioned, and she would have forfeited the work God wanted to DO in her life and the work He wanted to DISPLAY in her life.

"If you seek him, he will be found by you" (1 Chron. 28:9).

Chapter Ten

So That!

"Jesus looked her in the eye.
'Didn't I tell you that if you believed, you would see the glory of God?'"
John 11:40 (MSG)

Have you ever asked the Lord, "Why?" or had your plans, future, and dreams shattered?

I have asked the Lord (more times than I care to tell you about), "WHY did You do that? Why did You allow that?" Or, "Why didn't You do something? Why didn't You heal my mom of cancer? Why didn't You deliver my son from addiction?" (And the list goes on and on!)

As promised in the previous chapter, we are going to read about two more important words in God's Word. These two words give some explanation as to why God allows painful circumstances. They also have the power to change the trajectory of your life. Those two words are: *SO THAT!*

Read John 11 and take a fresh look at a familiar story. It's the story of Lazarus, Mary, and Martha, but this time we discover the explanation the Lord gives for WHY Lazarus died. Look for insights and observations in this story of WHY God did not intervene when they asked Him to. WHY did He allow this to happen?

To catch you up at this place in the story, Mary, Martha, and Lazarus were great friends of Jesus. Lazarus became very sick, so the two sisters sent a message to Jesus telling Him about it and calling for Him.

> *But when Jesus heard about it he said, "Lazarus's sickness will not end in death. No, it happened for the glory of God so that the Son of God will receive glory from this." So although Jesus loved Martha, Mary, and Lazarus, he stayed where he was for the next two days. Finally, he said to his disciples, "Let's go back to Judea." (John 11:4–7 NLT)*

There's so much here for us to see, but first it begs the question: Who does that? Who stays where they are after their friends have called them to come because the person they love has a life-threatening illness? Why the delay? Jesus loved this family. He knew they were hurting, but He did not respond immediately. He had a specific purpose in play. God's timing, especially His delays, may cause us to think He is not answering. In sorrow, His silence can strike at our emotions, and we are left feeling like, "He doesn't see me. He doesn't care about this." But His Word assures us—He promises us—He will meet all our needs according to His perfect schedule and purpose.

> *"And my God will supply every need of yours according to his riches in glory in Christ Jesus" (Phil. 4:19 ESV).*

We must patiently await His perfect time, for His perfect reason, SO THAT His intentions will be accomplished.

> *"And God is able to bless you abundantly, SO THAT in all things at all times, having all that you need, you will abound in every good work" (2 Cor. 9:8, emphasis mine).*

Please note how many times this Scripture says "ALL"! ALL things, at ALL times, having ALL that you need! Our natural thought process is to question what we don't understand and perhaps assume God is not doing anything. However, let's look at the supernatural process in the story the Lord planned, and let it help us better recognize how God might be at work in our circumstances as well.

According to John 11, there are TWO reasons given as to why the Lord delays and allows sorrow and suffering.

Reason #1: SO THAT the Son of God may **be glorified** (verse 4).

God allowed an occasion and set up a circumstance, a very painful circumstance, in their life SO THAT God would receive glory from it. It was a "glory opportunity"! Grief … yes. God's glory … yes!

The delay allowed Lazarus to die SO THAT his resurrection would be an unmistakable and undeniable miracle and display of God's power. His death served an important purpose.

Why? In two important words: *SO THAT!*

I am finally getting my head around the fact that Jesus would like to use MY life to display HIS glory! (My heart has been a little slower to get on board!) Why would I forfeit that kind of usefulness? The longer I walk with the Lord, the more I have come to realize that my life is apparently none of my business! I should stay out of it entirely!

Please note, the first reason had nothing to do with them. It had to do with God's glory being on display. However, reason number two had everything to do with them.

> *"Then Jesus told them plainly, 'Lazarus has died, and for your sake I am glad that I was not there, SO THAT you may believe. But let us go to him'" (John 11:14–15 ESV, emphasis mine).*

Reason #2: SO THAT **you** may believe (verse 15).

The Message Bible says it like this: "Then Jesus became explicit: 'Lazarus died. And I am glad for your sakes that I wasn't there. You're about to be given new grounds for believing. Now let's go to him.'"

I love this part: "You're about to be given new grounds for believing"! Your hard thing is the Lord creating new ground for you to believe! It's new ground to display His glory, to do something great, to show off in your life. God wants to demonstrate HIS power through OUR circumstances. He picked us for this problem.

Shocking circumstances have a way of shattering us. It can feel like a huge setback. But it's really a setup. It just depends on how you look at it. He is not so much into changing things as He is into changing the way you see things.

It's all about perspective. How we "see" what we can't see will help us believe that God is working in a realm that is not visible to us. Tony Evans says it like this: "If all you see is what you see, you will never see all that there is to be seen."[8]

Raise your hand out there if you have ever asked the Lord, "Why is this happening?" I will never forget an immediate lapse in my faith a few summers ago. My daughter called from a routine doctor's appointment to check on baby Abigail, whom she would be delivering in about seven weeks. I could hardly make out what she was saying through her sobs. Finally, she got it out: "Mom, please pray! I am in the doctor's office, and they cannot find her heartbeat." Within about thirty minutes it was confirmed. Abigail Jean had died in her womb. My immediate response to the Lord when I got off the phone was, "Why would You do that?"

At that time, we had two little grandsons. We had prayed for this little girl for two years! After several miscarriages, my daughter became pregnant. They waited for months before sharing the news with others. They waited before doing a gender reveal and even longer before preparing a beautiful little girl's room. But finally, we were ready for her arrival! And on a normal, routine day without any notice, our lives were shattered!

Lord, why would You do that?

I had to muster the hard words to myself and remind my heart one reason is SO THAT God would be glorified, and another reason is that it has created new ground for us to believe! Psalm 119:25 (NLT) says, "Revive me by your word." Verse 28 tells us, "I weep with sorrow; encourage me by your word."

---

8   Tony Evans, *Victory in Spiritual Warfare: Outfitting Yourself for the Battle* (Harvest House Publishers, 2011).

I am learning:

- Do not demand explanations.
- Do not assume you know the plan.
- Do not try to work your own outcome.
- And, for heaven's sake, do not interrupt God's work with your argument!

> *"I have told you all this SO THAT you may have peace in me. Here on earth you will have many trials and sorrows. But take heart, because I have overcome the world" (John 16:33 NLT).*

Your discontent, personal preferences, and impatience is going to get you sidetracked. And guess where the devil would like you to be? Sidetracked—in the ditch, grumbling and complaining about how unfair it all is. I mentioned this in a previous chapter but need to remind us again to focus on the *unfolding* of it all, not the unfairness of it all.

Our emotional and mental wellness might be riding on our response to the Lord when life-shattering things happen. (In a later chapter, I will share "Ten Ways to Train Your Brain.")

Sidetracked— in the ditch, grumbling and complaining about how unfair it all is.

Later, in John 11:40 (MSG), the Bible says, "Jesus looked her in the eye. 'Didn't I tell you that **IF YOU** believed, you would see the glory of God?'" (emphasis mine).

"IF YOU" requires a response. This is part of your action plan.

I love the Lord's personal attention to her. There was a seed in her sorrow that the Lord wanted to plant. I wonder what adjustments she had to make in her life to bring that seed to a huge harvest. Don't let sorrow hinder sowing!

> *"And blessed is she that believed: for there shall be a performance of those things which were told her from the Lord" (Luke 1:45 KJV).*

When we don't see His activity and when we don't feel His presence, we can still be assured of His faithfulness. Great is His faithfulness! Psalm 90:12 (CSB) says, "Teach us to number our days carefully SO THAT we may develop wisdom in our hearts" (emphasis mine). That means to make the most of your time, your days, and your circumstances … ALL of them!

> *"Above all, be strong and very courageous to observe carefully the whole instruction…. . Do not turn from it to the right or the left, SO THAT you will have success wherever you go" (Josh. 1:7 CSB, emphasis mine).*

Focus Verse

> *"Jesus looked her in the eye. 'Didn't I tell you that if you believed, you would see the glory of God?'" (John 11:40 MSG).*

Connecting the Dots

The story of Mary, Martha, and Lazarus is about:

- Our response to crisis.
- Waiting on the Lord.
- Believing the Lord.
- Trusting the Lord.
- Seeing God's purpose and power.
- Watching God at work in our lives for His glory.

Make It Personal

I want to close this chapter with a favorite chorus that helps me align my emotions to the will of God. I hope it is familiar to you. Take a moment, sit still, and sing this to the Lord as a prayer of commitment.

"Lord Be Glorified" by Bob Kilpatrick, The Maranatha! Singers:[9]

In my life, Lord
Be glorified, be glorified
In my life, Lord
Be glorified today ...

In my heart, Lord

Be glorified, be glorified

In my heart, Lord

Be glorified today

... for He [God] Himself has said, I will not in any way fail you nor give you up nor leave you without support. [I will] not, [I will] not, [I will] not in any degree leave you helpless nor forsake nor let [you] down (relax My hold on you)! [Assuredly not!] (Hebrews 13:5 AMPC)

---

9   Bob Kilpatrick, The Maranatha! Singers, "Lord Be Glorified," *Praise III*, 1979.

Chapter Eleven

Found Faithful

"His master said to him,
'Well done, good and faithful servant.
You have been faithful.'"
Matthew 25:21 (ESV)

I pray this chapter will be extremely beneficial and yield much fruit in your life. The principles we are learning today have altered my perspective on what it means to finish strong!

For years I have used that phrase: "Finish strong!" I have encouraged others to finish strong and have said to the Lord I want to finish strong. The older I get, the deeper my desire to do this becomes. I want to hear the words, "Well done, good and faithful servant!" But often, I think what I will hear is … "WELL!?!?! Well, what were you thinking? Well, what happened to you today? Well, why did you act that way or say those words or watch that show?"

To borrow a phrase from the Millennial generation, "What does that even mean?"

What does it mean to finish strong? God's Word explains it in a story, so let's find out what it means. Look in your Bible in Matthew 25 and also Luke 19.

These are two stories that are referred to as the Parable of the Talents. Scholars believe these are two different parables and although they have some similarities in word usage, they have key elements that are different. Jesus would sometimes modify this teaching to fit different situations and emphasize different truths to match the current situation. But the main principles in these stories are the same and if we implement them in our lives, we too will be "found faithful"!

Here's the story—picture it in your mind as it plays out. Pay close attention to details. Make some mental and spiritual observations. Also think about what you might do in this situation. If this is a familiar story to you, ask the Lord for fresh insight and new perspective.

Read Matthew 25:14–30 (NLT):

Parable of the Three Servants

Again, the Kingdom of Heaven can be illustrated by the story of a man going on a long trip. He called together his servants and entrusted his money to them while he was gone. He gave five bags of silver to one, two bags of silver to another, and one bag of silver to the last—dividing it in proportion to their abilities. He then left on his trip. The servant who received the five bags of silver began to invest the money and earned five more. The servant with two bags of silver also went to work and earned two more. But the servant who received the one bag of silver dug a hole in the ground and hid the master's money.

After a long time their master returned from his trip and called them to give an account of how they had used his money. The servant to whom he had entrusted the five bags of silver came forward with five more and said, "Master, you gave me five bags of silver to invest, and I have earned five more." The master was full of praise. "Well done, my good and faithful servant. You have been faithful in handling this small amount, so now I will give you many more responsibilities. Let's celebrate together!"

The servant who had received the two bags of silver came forward and said, "Master, you gave me two bags of silver to invest, and I have earned two more." The master said, "Well done, my good and faithful servant. You have been faithful in handling this small amount, so now I will give you many more responsibilities. Let's celebrate together!"

> *Then the servant with the one bag of silver came and said, "Master, I knew you were a harsh man, harvesting crops you didn't plant and gathering crops you didn't cultivate. I was afraid I would lose your money, so I hid it in the earth. Look, here is your money back." But the master replied, "You wicked and lazy servant! If you knew I harvested crops I didn't plant and gathered crops I didn't cultivate, why didn't you deposit my money in the bank? At least I could have gotten some interest on it." Then he ordered, "Take the money from this servant, and give it to the one with the ten bags of silver. To those who use well what they are given, even more will be given, and they will have an abundance. But from those who do nothing, even what little they have will be taken away. Now throw this useless servant into outer darkness, where there will be weeping and gnashing of teeth."*

Oh! There is so much to unpack here. Let's hit some high points and make some personal application.

In this parable, God teaches that what we invest on earth will have rewards in heaven.

Looking back at the story …

What was given?

The answer is not just money.

They were given something of value (talents, minas, resources, gifts).

Think deeper—what are some valuable things we have been given from the Lord?

We've been given responsibilities, experiences, assignments, skills, talents. All of these are very valuable to the Lord. And one of the most important things that they, and we, have been given is time.

Why was it given?

Matthew 25:27 (NIV) indicates it was given to invest, and to grow.

How was it given?

It was given with a PURPOSE! It was given according to their abilities: "… dividing it in proportion to their abilities" (Matt. 25:15 NLT).

And may I please add that it was not given for them to compare to each other.

What did each one do with what was given to them?

The first servant put the pedal to the metal and *began immediately* to invest it.

> # Even the hard stuff can yield an abundance when we are faithful.

Two of them invested what was entrusted to them. They used it, they grew it, and it became more valuable to the master. This pleased the master; he loved that!

Verse 21 (NLT) says, "The master was full of praise. 'Well done, my good and faithful servant. You have been faithful.'" And there were rewards from the master.

Faithfulness has rewards!

Faithfulness is not just about beliefs or intentions. It is measured by action that bears fruit. There are rewards for faithfulness.

Faith requires action!

The teaching from this passage is to use what the Lord has given—what the Lord has entrusted to you. For some of us, what the Lord has given us is inoperative, and you must purposefully engage it. You CAN use cancer, the death of a loved one, a prodigal child, and an unexpected divorce to glorify God. Even the hard stuff can yield an abundance when we are faithful.

"You crown the year with a bountiful harvest; even the hard pathways overflow with abundance" (Ps. 65:11 NLT).

The Bible tells us that Timothy was a godly guy. But two times Paul had to write to him and admonish him to get with the program and use the gifts God had given him. Timothy apparently was using excuses rather than using his gifts. God has given us something that He wants us to use for His kingdom. The question is, will we?

Work the program!

"Moreover, it is required of stewards that they be found faithful" (1 Cor. 4:2 ESV).

I want to talk about the last servant, the one who didn't do so well. The first two began immediately, they wasted no time, and they gave no excuses. My heart always goes out to the one that struggles to get it right. The one who couldn't seem to produce what the Lord wanted. I was truly pulling for this one in my study time.

Why, according to God's Word, did he do nothing?

The Bible says in verse 25 (NLT), "I was afraid." FEAR caused him to do nothing with what God had given. What might he have been afraid of? (Think about how fear works in your life.)

- Afraid of what might happen.
- Afraid it might not work out.
- Afraid to mess it up.
- Afraid of failure in the eyes of others.

Has anyone but me been afraid of what people might think or say? I wonder, have they tried many times before and failed? Maybe they listened to people around them that said, "You never get things right." Perhaps they listened to their own voice saying, "Don't even try!"

Who knows what they have been through?

The Lord gave the last servant a little—just one bag. (Remember, it was in proportion to their abilities.) Don't be tempted to think: *I have so little. What difference could it make?*

If you are a young person or an old person, a single mom, a widow, working a crazy job, or feel like you don't have time, this story teaches us that we must invest what was entrusted.

It is not: What amount was given? It is: What did you do with the amount?

I love my *Charles Spurgeon Study Bible*. Here are his thoughts about this story:

- A great deal of unfaithfulness is caused by endeavoring to please people.
- Also, we injure our faithfulness by idling, trifling, growing careless, or leaving our hearts out of our work.
- Further, we prove ourselves unfaithful by misusing our gift.
- And we become unfaithful stewards by complaining about whatever is wrong with our fellow servants.[10]

I shudder to think how many times I have injured my faithfulness! Lord, forgive me!

Are any of these issues playing out in your life?

So, what did the last servant do with what he was given? He hid it. He was afraid he would lose it.

So. He. Did. Nothing. He didn't even try. He may have had his reason, his excuses, his rationalizations. But they all caused him to disobey the Lord and forfeit the blessings and rewards that were awaiting his obedience.

I can picture in my mind what he was probably saying: "I didn't double it, but I didn't lose it! See, I still have it." And what he had was then taken away from him, because he failed to use it.

---

10   Charles Spurgeon, *The CSB Spurgeon Study Bible*, ed. Alistair Begg (Holman Bible Publisher, 2017).

Fears and feelings will keep you from being faithful!

Think back to chapter three: Don't. Do. Nothing! Doing nothing is considered unfaithful. His fear led to disobedience.

Don't hide your gift.

This story reveals the severe consequence of the servant who did nothing. The consequences of being unfaithful are life-changing! God called him foolish, wicked, and lazy.

Think back to the FIRST command we were given in Scripture … all the way back to Adam and Eve. The first command: "Be fruitful and multiply" (Gen. 1:28 NLT).

I need you to hear this please: The Lord has expectations of you! Like it or not, you have a divine purpose. Everything you've been through is useful!

There are consequences for neglect and laziness.

And one more observation: The last servant said, "Master, I knew you were a harsh man" (Matt. 25:24 NLT).

Where did that come from? How and why did he conclude that the master who JUST GAVE HIM money was so harsh and hard? He wasn't a harsh man. He gave them all a **gift**, then gave them a **chance**, then gave them **time,** and then rewarded them generously and compassionately. Where's the harshness? Somewhere along the way, he developed the wrong attitude about his master. Also, it doesn't appear he knew his master very well. What about you? How well do you know your Master?

So, two servants received a "well done" from the master. They were FOUND FAITHFUL!

What about you? What might the Lord say to you?

You have been found _____?

The master did not say to them, "You have been found very nice, really smart, well connected, very influential, well educated, helpful, sweet, well liked." He said, "You have been faithful"!

And I believe it's what the Lord is asking for of us today—to be *found faithful*!

What has the Lord entrusted to you?

A home, education, experiences, influence, job, opportunities, common sense, finances, creative abilities, communication/writing skills? One thing He has given all of us is a mouth. We can use our words to invest for Him. We might need to help others recognize what they've been given.

> # We can use our words to invest for Him.

He has given us the whole worldwide web to communicate on! Not just the good things; the Lord reminded me, He has entrusted me with things I was likely to hide. There are difficult things that He wants me to use—seasons of suffering, for example. I was entrusted with a prodigal. Some of you have been entrusted with cancer, with a special-needs child, with physical difficulties, medical issues, etc.

What have you done with it? Did you hide it because you were afraid? Were you afraid of what people might say or think?

Hardships and difficulties need to be invested.

You can become a faithful servant by serving a faithful God. Each of us will be held accountable for how we lived and used what God entrusted to us. Therefore, leverage your stuff (your time, money, resources, abilities, experiences, wisdom, words, personality, etc.) for maximum impact!

Focus Verse

"His master said to him, 'Well done, good and faithful servant. You have been faithful'"
(Matt. 25:21 ESV).

Connecting the Dots

The story of a master and three servants teaches us that:

- Faithfulness is pleasing to the Lord.
- Fear limits our God-given ability.
- We are all entrusted with a gift from God to use for His glory.

Make It Personal

The following are five additional references in God's Word about being faithful. I hope you will take some time and study through these people and their stories.

How are you found faithful?

1. You can be faithful in the **land of affliction**. "For God has made me fruitful in the land of my affliction" (Gen. 41:52 ESV).
2. You can be faithful in a **famine**. The Shunammite woman lost everything in a famine. But she decided to listen to the Lord, follow His direction, and she received back NOT ONLY what she lost but also the value of what was lost (see 2 Kings 8).
3. You can be faithful in the **wilderness**. Joshua was faithful in his wilderness season. He inquired of the Lord about every battle and committed to follow the Lord in every step.
4. You can be faithful through **transition**. Joseph went from the pit to the prison to the palace. He dealt with false accusations, purity, and pride, but always yielded to providence of God.

5. You can be faithful in your **suffering**. In Acts 16, Paul and Silas were worshiping and praying while they were sitting in a jail cell, haven been severely beaten, betrayed for doing what the Lord had asked them to do. It was not fair! But other prisoners were watching and were delivered as a result of their faith.

"Be joyful in hope, patient in affliction, faithful in prayer" (Rom. 12:12).

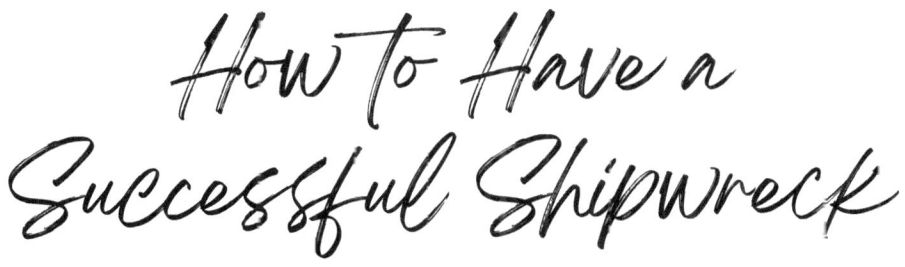

Chapter Twelve

How To Have a Successful Shipwreck

> *"So take courage! For I believe God. It will be just as he said."*
> Acts 27:25 (NLT)

Lord, I pray Your Word would redirect our thoughts, plans, and priorities. Help us, Father, to see You in the midst of our storm and throw overboard all nonessentials. We anchor ourselves in Your Word so that we will not abandon hope. Amen.

Read Acts 27:1–26.

Pay close attention to the details of the story. Focus. Make some observations. Let these words be a compass to you as you navigate storms in life.

Here is the bottom line of this story. Paul was being faithful and obedient, yet he was shipwrecked. Seems to me that people serving the Lord and being faithful and obedient should be successful, not shipwrecked. But the Lord didn't ask my opinion. Now, let's unpack the whole story where you can see that the Lord was getting ready to do a great thing in Paul's life, and it's a good thing he didn't stop at the great tragedy.

There is a small word that may seem unimportant in the first verse that is easy to skip because it is a normal part of our vocabulary. But this is why in-depth Bible study is important; it causes you to pause and look up such words.

It's the word *time*. Verse 1 (NLT) says, "When the time came …" Another translation (KJV) says, "And when it was determined …" This means there was a definite purpose in play AT THIS TIME.

It means it was:

- A moment of indeterminate time in which something special happens.
- A passing instant when an opening appears which must be driven through with force if success is to be achieved.
- The appointed time in the purpose of God.
- A time in which God acts.

I think the Lord may have been saying, "Paul … IT'S TIME!" It's time.

I think the Lord might be saying the same thing to us as well. It's time. It's time to get something great underway.

Let's take some time to study through the story and see what lessons you can pull out. Here are some I was able to find:

Lessons for Successful SHIPWRECKS

- God appoints shipwrecks. God wanted Paul shipwrecked for His own good reasons.
- Sometimes, even though we are faithful, obedient, and trying to do what is right, we will be shipwrecked.
- Do you need to alter your course?
- Are there things you need to throw overboard that are delaying your progress?
- The storm is not hindering your destiny; it's helping it with redirection.
- Don't give up (see verse 15).
- Don't abandon hope (see verse 20).
- Faith will make you calm. When everyone else wanted to "jump ship," Paul remained calm because he knew to whom he belonged, and he knew whom he served. God was beside him, as he is you! (See verse 23.)

- Anchor yourself to God's Word (see verse 24).
- Allow God to encourage you. Then encourage others.
- It's not what you know but what you obey that determines your destiny.
- Pray for providence!
  - Providence: God's divine care, control, and guidance over your life, situations, and circumstances, making you ready for future events (definition from an 1812 dictionary).
- Take courage! Believe God! (See verse 25.)
- It was just as God said: They were shipwrecked, and they survived (as will you) (see verse 26).
- You might have to be shipwrecked but you do not have to stay shipwrecked!
- This shipwreck set into motion a series of circumstances that changed the lives of many, many people and set some miracles in motion.
- Your shipwreck is for a purpose that you cannot see while the winds are raging and your ship is battered.

Paul's behavior was brave and inspiring in the midst of a storm that most people would not survive. His dependence was on the Lord. His focus was on the One who walks on water during a storm. His energy and ears were directed to hearing the voice of the Lord. And with that, his perspective changed.

If you keep reading in chapter 28 of Acts, you will discover five or six incredible, miraculous things that could not have happened had Paul and his people not been shipwrecked. I am tempted to say that shipwreck HAD TO HAPPEN! Read through it and make a list of all the positive things and miracles that occurred as a result of this shipwreck.

God caused extraordinary ministry to come from his extraordinary tragedy.

As I mentioned in a previous chapter, our shipwreck happened on October 16, 2009, when two police officers walked into our home and arrested our son, Jarrad. He had been a prodigal in our home for about five years. He began to self-medicate when our family faced several tragic things in a short period of time. His drug addiction had severe consequences.

I knew nothing about prison. I had no idea what inmates and their families go through. That world and those needs were not on my radar and apparently that was a problem for the Lord, because it quickly became my world. As a result, prison ministry to women began at Prestonwood Baptist Church. My church, Green Acres Baptist Church, has been faithfully going to prisons for years and several other churches are participating. Space does not allow me to share the unbelievable things we have seen the Lord do through prison ministry. As I write this, we currently have thirty-six women scheduled to be baptized in a prison.

But I just have to tell you this one story about a sweet woman and how God changed her life. There are many more details than I can give but here is the heart of the story.

The storms in your life have purpose.

When we began prison ministry in Dallas, Texas, we were only allowed to visit the faith-based pods. We asked the warden if we could bring Bibles for the inmates and he harshly refused our request. So, I asked our prayer team to start praying and asking the Lord to help us get Bibles into this prison. About three weeks later I asked him again, if we could please bring Bib—and before I could finish my sentence, he said, "OKAY, OKAY! Go ahead and bring the Bibles in." (I am quite certain the Lord had gotten to him!)

We brought Bibles, and the women went crazy over them! Not long afterwards we realized they needed help working through hardships and difficulties in their lives and we wanted them to know and understand that God wanted to use those to strengthen them and build them up. Beth Moore had just released a Bible study on James, so I asked the warden if we could please bring those in and he harshly said, "Absolutely not!" (I thought to myself, "Really, you want to do this with me again?") So, I got the prayer team involved. Three weeks later I asked him again and he said, "Sure."

I will never forget the day we brought the Bible studies into prison. Those women cried, some danced, and some knelt down on the dirty floor and thanked the Lord. But there was one small, frail, older woman that had a different response. See, in all the times we had come to her pod, she never participated in Bible study. She always stood behind a big pole in the room and never said a word and never looked our direction. Some other inmates told me they thought she didn't speak English and that I should leave her alone.

That day we of course gave her the James Bible study as well. She took it and went back to stand behind the pole. After our celebration we began looking through the workbook and explaining how to do the study of James. Then that woman stepped out from behind the pole and said, "May I say something?" I was stunned. The girl in front of me said, "We didn't know she could speak English!"

I said, "Yes, ma'am, what would you like to say?" She said, "I was excited to get this book. I've never had a Bible study before. I thought it might help me get my life on track. But then the voice inside me said, 'You're not going to learn anything because you can't read!'"

I've never been speechless a day in my life except that day at that moment. Before I could say anything, the lady on the second row said, "I'm a fourth grade English teacher. I'm going to teach you how to read!"

I said, "Take that, devil!"

Oh, I have so many stories of God's intervention in the lives of women in prison.

We need to live our lives in such a way as to make the devil sorry he messed with us in the first place. I need you to know that none of this happened because Debbie Stuart had a great idea to start prison ministry. It happened because Debbie Stuart had the shipwreck of a lifetime and thought she would not survive!

The storms in your life have purpose. The book of James in the Bible instructs us that hardships are used by God to develop perseverance and endurance. I read this anonymous poem many years ago and the Lord often brings it to my mind whenever I tend to complain and whine.

When God wants to drill a man
And thrill a man
And skill a man
When God wants to mold a man
To play the noblest part

When He yearns with all His heart
To create so great and bold a man
That all the world shall be amazed
Watch His methods, watch His ways!

How He ruthlessly perfects
Whom He royally elects!
How He hammers him and hurts him
And with mighty blows converts him

Into trial shapes of clay which
Only God understands
While His tortured heart is crying
And He lifts beseeching hands!

How He bends but never breaks
When His good He undertakes
How He uses whom He chooses
And which every purpose fuses Him
By every act induces Him
To try His splendor out
God knows what He's about

Don't WASTE your shipwreck! WAIT on the purposes of God to be fulfilled!

"Be joyful in hope, patient in affliction, faithful in prayer" (Rom. 12:12).

One morning while praying through our devastating shipwreck, my prayers *may have* turned from praying to whining. I was so overwhelmed with all that was happening I didn't even know how to pray. I could not find words to articulate what I felt, what I needed, and what I believed. I begged God to intervene and end this living nightmare. I would do anything. (Another lesson from storms—they make you desperate!) While studying several different passages, these are

Don't WASTE your shipwreck!

the words I heard the Lord clearly speak in my heart. I memorized them and quote them often when I find myself overwhelmed.

The Lord said to me, "When you pray to be delivered from your difficulties and I do so, you are only being rescued, not victorious. I am trying to train you to be armed, equipped, and disciplined for the adversary, but you keep trying to end the training process. I want you to WIN this, Debbie, not be excused from it!"

Think on that for a moment. Read it again.

That is notecard-worthy, my friend. It's a word I believe He is speaking to anyone who has ever begged for God's intervention and to end the nightmare and suffering. To beg the Lord to rescue you from pain and distress will only make you weak, spoiled, and spiritually unresponsive.

I cannot promise you that in this storm everything will be okay, but I can promise you that YOU will be okay if you will anchor yourself to the Word of God.

Katherine Wolf, author of *Hope Heals*, states in her recent book, *Treasures in the Dark*, "Suffering is not the end of my story. Pain and joy can coexist. New life always begins with the end of an old life. My hope is not in any good gift but in the Giver of every good gift."[11]

> *"This hope we have as an anchor of the soul, both sure and steadfast"* (Heb. 6:19 NKJV).

---

11   Katherine Wolf, *Treasures in the Dark: 90 Reflections on Finding Bright Hope Hidden in the Hurting* (Thomas Nelson, 2024).

"You are a refuge from the storm and a shelter from the heat" (Isa. 25:4 NLT).

"He who sows righteousness will have a sure reward" (Prov. 11:18 NKJV).

"The LORD your God in your midst, the Mighty One, will save; He will rejoice over you with gladness, He will quiet you with His love, He will rejoice over you with singing" (Zeph. 3:17 NKJV).

Focus Verse

"So take courage! For I believe God. It will be just as he said" (Acts 27:25 NLT).

Connecting the Dots

Courage. How do we *take* courage? Looking at other Bible translations gives us a clue. Instead of "take courage," the KJV says, "Be of good cheer," and the ESV says to "take heart." *Take heart* means to keep up your courage, to put in good spirits, and to make cheerful. These are all action statements. Taking courage is something we do that we can control. It comes from the heart training the mind to be strong and cheerful no matter the circumstances. Sometimes this is easier said than done, I know. But the fact that it begins in the heart tells me our courage is from Jesus. Ask Him for it and He will give it. Then hang on to it—keep it up no matter what.

Make It Personal

Are your trusting the Lord and asking Him to turn your tragedy into a triumph, your obstacles into opportunities, and your challenges into channels for Him to work?

_____

_____

Is there any "extra baggage" you need to throw overboard?

_____

_____

Have you recklessly taken over as captain of your own ship?

_____

_____

Have any of your divine assignments taken a turn toward your personal interests?

_____

_____

Do you have difficulty being content with your current circumstances? Cultivate a thankful spirit this week.

_____

_____

Chapter Thirteen

Turning Points and Transitions

Three Essential Actions We Must Take to Move Forward in Faith

"May the God of hope fill you with all joy and peace as you trust in him, so that you may overflow with hope by the power of the Holy Spirit."
Romans 15:13 (NIV)

This is the only chapter I feel the need to give a subtitle to. It's going to be very action-oriented: "Turning Points and Transitions: Three Essential Actions We Must Take to Move Forward in Faith." It intentionally comes right after the shipwreck message.

I believe our shipwrecks offer new opportunities for believing God and offer an open door for action. They are turning points and defining moments in our lives. In Acts 27, there is a huge crossroad in Paul's life. He was headed one direction, and an unexpected storm blew him off course, away from his plan, in a different direction.

Acts 27:15 (NLT) says, "The sailors couldn't turn the ship into the wind, so they gave up." They. Gave. Up. Perhaps thoughts like this flooded their minds: *This is the worst thing ever. Nothing good is coming out of this. It is so unfair. We will never survive.* This storm then produced a shipwreck. They hit a crisis. The men on the boat became afraid;

they didn't know what to do, they had no light, no direction, and no control. They were exhausted and overwhelmed. The Bible says some tried to jump ship. (I may have figuratively tried to jump ship in a few of my storms!)

Then comes one of the saddest Scriptures in all the Bible: "All hope was gone" (Acts 27:20 NLT).

Then God showed up! Many times in my life I have noticed that when I lost hope … God showed up! He gave instructions and they ended up having a successful shipwreck. That sounds like an oxymoron—"a successful shipwreck." Let's look at how.

The morning Jarrad was arrested, I had spent time with the Lord in my usual place at my usual time. Officers gave my husband a card with a number to call. As he did that, I ran into my Bible study room where I had just met with the Lord. I had just prayed for the deliverance of my son and for God to turn his life around. I threw myself on the chair where I had knelt to pray and proclaimed, "This is the worst thing that could have ever happened to him! Why didn't You deliver my son? I have watched You deliver other people's children. Why wouldn't You deliver mine?"

At that moment, in my spirit, I heard the Lord say, "I just did!"

See, here's Debbie Stuart's problem: I had a preconceived idea of what deliverance ought to look like! I had a good plan about his turn-around, and it didn't involve us being shipwrecked and him going to prison.

Anybody with me on developing their own awesome plan?

Let's talk through some action steps in order to get to a successful shipwreck. I believe the foundation is found in Act 27:25: Take courage and believe God. From the story of Paul's shipwreck comes our three essential actions!

Action Step #1: Get a Grip on HOPE!

God is with you in the storm. Do not abandon hope. You are never without hope. His presence gives peace to panic! There is hope and hope has a name—it's Jesus Christ, and I hope you know Him.

Make hope a habit. It's not so much a feeling as it is a habit.

Feed hope and starve fear, anxiety, worry, questions, doubts, and hopelessness.

There are no hopeless situations—only people who have lost hope.

Hope has been defined as:

- Confident expectation of better days ahead. This will get better and, if you believe God's Word is true, something good will grow from this.
- Optimistic assurance that something will be fulfilled.

Romans 15:4 says, "For everything that was written in the past was written to teach us, so that through the endurance taught in the Scriptures and the encouragement they provide we might have hope."

Hebrews 10:23 says, "Let us hold unswervingly to the hope we profess, for he who promised is faithful."

Katherine Wolf stated, "The habit and practice of hope carried me when the feeling of hope failed me."[12]

Romans 5:3–5 (NLT) says:

> *We can rejoice, too, when we run into problems and trials, for we know that they help us develop endurance. And endurance develops strength of character, and character strengthens our confident hope of salvation. And this hope will not lead to disappointment. For we know how dearly God loves us, because he has given us the Holy Spirit to fill our hearts with his love.*

---

12   Katherine Wolf, *Treasures in the Dark: 90 Reflections on Finding Bright Hope Hidden in the Hurting* (Thomas Nelson, 2024).

Romans 5:2–5 from *The Message* Bible says:

> *We find ourselves standing where we always hoped we might stand—out in the wide open spaces of God's grace and glory, standing tall and shouting our praise. There's more to come: We continue to shout our praise even when we're hemmed in with troubles, because we know how troubles can develop passionate patience in us, and how that patience in turn forges the tempered steel of virtue, keeping us alert for whatever God will do next. In alert expectancy such as this, we're never left feeling shortchanged. Quite the contrary—we can't round up enough containers to hold everything God generously pours into our lives through the Holy Spirit!*

It's not always strength, strategy, or even grit that gets you through difficulty, hardship, or suffering—it's hope. It is a confident expectation rooted in the goodness and faithfulness of God.

> **It's not always strength, strategy, or even grit that gets you through difficulty, hardship, or suffering—it's hope.**

Think for a moment. What hinders hope in your life? What helps hope?

Paul talked the guys out of jumping ship. He called them together and encouraged them, basically saying, "Hey, don't quit! This is what the Lord said.…" The best thing you can do for someone is help them turn the page and help them through a storm. You might have to BE shipwrecked, but you don't have to STAY shipwrecked.

Your obedience matters! Especially in a crisis.

Lamentations 3:19–25 (MSG) says:

It's a Good Thing to Hope for Help from GOD

> *I'll never forget the trouble, the utter lostness, the taste of ashes, the poison I've swallowed. I remember it all—oh, how well I remember—the feeling of hitting the bottom. But there's one other thing I remember, and*

remembering, I keep a grip on hope: GOD's loyal love couldn't have run out, his merciful love couldn't have dried up. They're created new every morning. How great your faithfulness! I'm sticking with GOD (I say it over and over). He's all I've got left. GOD proves to be good to the man who passionately waits, to the woman who diligently seeks. It's a good thing to quietly hope, quietly hope for help from GOD. It's a good thing when you're young to stick it out through the hard times. When life is heavy and hard to take, go off by yourself. Enter the silence. Bow in prayer. Don't ask questions: Wait for hope to appear. Don't run from trouble. Take it full-face. The "worst" is never the worst. Why? Because the Master won't ever walk out and fail to return. If he works severely, he also works tenderly. His stockpiles of loyal love are immense. He takes no pleasure in making life hard, in throwing roadblocks in the way.

Our first action step: Get a grip on hope! Get your hands on God's Word and put yourself in His presence. This leads right into our second action step.

Action Step #2: Anchor Yourself in God's Word!

In the story, part of the instruction God gave Paul was to throw out anchors. Throwing out anchors helps minimize the damage and stabilize the vessel.

"Guide me in your truth and teach me, for you are God my Savior, and my hope is in you all day long" (Ps. 25:5). This is the foundational anchor—God's Word—out of which we have stabilizing anchors.

What are the rocks in your life you fear will break you apart?

Consider these four anchors to help stabilize and anchor your life:

1. **Obedience**. In times of trial, you lean in, walk closer, and listen carefully.
2. **Courage**. Be brave! Hide yourself in the shadow of the Almighty. Do hard things.
3. **Believe**. "For I know whom I have believed … that He is able" (2 Tim. 1:12 ESV). Also, get around believers!

4. **Thanksgiving**. Develop a heart of gratitude. Psalm 65:11 (NLT) says, "You crown the year with a bountiful harvest; even the hard pathways overflow with abundance."

   "Blessed is the man who trusts in the LORD, and whose hope is the LORD" *(Jer. 7:7 NKJV).*

Charles Spurgeon said, "I have learned to kiss the waves that throw me up against the Rock of Ages."

So, anchor yourself in God's Word. Here's some ways you can do that:

- Make a daily habit. As I say: "Twenty Minutes a Day for the Rest of Your Life!"
- Make room for the Lord. We make room for everything else in our lives. We've made room for 147 apps, and all the social media platforms: Facebook, Instagram, Netflix, Instant Messenger, Twitter (now X), etc. (I told someone awhile back—someone needs to put them all together and call it "XTwitface" or something!)

And think about this: At Christmas we share the Christmas story. But here's an important part of the story that we have been leaving out that I want you to PUT in this year. Mary and Joseph came to Bethlehem because Jesus was about to be born. Most often, we say something like this: "They came to Bethlehem and Jesus was born in a manger." However, FIRST, they went from place to place, from house to house, knocking on doors. And what was said when they were looking for room for Jesus? "WE HAVE NO ROOM!"

> **Make sure your family knows that you are making room for the Lord.**

From the beginning we have told Jesus: "We have no room." Make sure your family knows that you are making room for the Lord. It doesn't mean life gets easier; it means you're holding onto something stronger.

Consider the direction in these Scriptures (my paraphrase):

- Hope grounded in Christ does not disappoint (see Romans 5:5).
- We have this hope as an anchor, steadfast and sure (see Hebrews 6:19).
- Put God's Word into practice (see Psalm 119:34).
- The unfolding of your Word gives light (see Psalm 119:130).

So, we've covered:

- Action Step #1: Get a Grip on Hope
- Action Step #2: Anchor Yourself in God's Word

And Action Step #3 is …

Action Step #3: Take Courage and Believe God (from Acts 27:25)

Having hope will give you courage. That speaks to our first action step: Get a grip on hope.

Five Ways to Guard Against Hopelessness

1. Make a choice! (Verbally)
   Even though the fig trees have no blossoms, and there are no grapes on the vines; even though the olive crop fails, and the fields lie empty and barren; even though the flocks die in the fields, and the cattle barns are empty, yet I will rejoice in the Lord! I will be joyful in the God of my salvation! The Sovereign Lord is my strength! He makes me as surefooted as a deer, able to tread upon the heights. (Habakkuk 3:17–19 NLT)

2. Take a stand! (Physically, Practically)
   Lamentations 3:24 (NLT) says, "I say to myself, 'The LORD is my inheritance; therefore, I will hope in him!'"

3. Shift your focus! (Mentally)
   Psalm 27:13 (NKJV) says, "I would have lost heart, unless I had believed that I would see the goodness of the LORD in the land of the living."

4. Lean on truth. (Spiritually)
    Psalm 119:130 (NIV) says, "The unfolding of your words gives light; it gives understanding to the simple."

5. Thank the Lord. (Emotionally)
    I will praise the LORD at all times. I will constantly speak his praises. I will boast only in the LORD; let all who are helpless take heart. Come, let us tell of the LORD's greatness; let us exalt his name together. I prayed to the LORD, and he answered me. He freed me from all my fears. Those who look to him for help will be radiant with joy; no shadow of shame will darken their faces. In my desperation I prayed, and the LORD listened; he saved me from all my troubles. For the angel of the LORD is a guard; he surrounds and defends all who fear him. Taste and see that the LORD is good. Oh, the joys of those who take refuge in him! (Psalm 34:1–8 NLT)

He will "transform the Valley of Trouble into a gateway of hope" (Hosea 2:15 NLT).

Even when the cattle barns are empty and no grapes are on the vine. So, when things aren't great, we still have a choice to make.

When Jarrad was incarcerated, I stayed closely connected to Bill Glass's prison ministry. This is a story a representative shared at a ministry fundraiser about a man incarcerated in Virginia. I believe his name was Joe. He had served twenty years, and he was about a week away from parole. He had led many Bible studies and led many men to Christ during his incarceration. But they had limited him to sharing Bibles with only his one pod where he was housed.

Many men were very happy about his upcoming freedom—but not everyone. One man hated him for his love for the Lord, and he planted drugs in his cell. The next day they were found, and although the guards knew they were not his (they knew his character and reputation), prison process and procedures required them to write it up and report it. His parole was immediately revoked; he was given additional time and sent to maximum security for the violation.

His friends were very upset and threated harm against the man who planted the drugs. But Joe sent word to forgive him and show him the love of Christ (as they had been taught). Joe sent word to his family about what had happened, that he was being moved to maximum security, and to pray for those men as he was hopeful to start Bible studies there and get them some Bibles.

Joe's mom wrote him a letter, and she shared that for years she had been praying that her son could minister to more men than just those in his pod. So, her prayers had been answered. A revival broke out in that prison because of this whole ordeal. The man who planted the drugs was saved and confessed to officers what he had done. Shortly thereafter, Joe was released on parole. Yet Bible study in maximum security kept growing as a result of Joe being there.

> *"'You shall know that I have done nothing without cause ...' says the Lord God" (Ezek. 14:23 NKJV).*

> *"'For I know the plans I have for you,' declares the Lord, 'plans to prosper you and not to harm you, plans to give you a hope and a future'" (Jer. 29:11).*

But wait, there's more:

Verse 12 says, "Then you will call on me and come and pray to me, and I will listen to you."

Verse 13 says, "You will seek me and find me when you seek me with all your heart."

Our action steps are:

1. Get a Grip on Hope
2. Anchor Yourself in God's Word
3. Take Courage and Believe God

Lastly, hope when answers are delayed.

Psalm 62:5–8 (NLT) says:

> *Let all that I am wait quietly before God, for my hope is in him. He alone is my rock and my salvation, my fortress where I will not be shaken. My victory and honor come from God alone. He is my refuge, a rock where no*

enemy can reach me. O my people, trust in him at all times. Pour out your
heart to him, for God is our refuge.

Sometimes the only thing hope can do is help us wait. Isaiah 40:31
(NKJV) says, "But those who wait on the LORD shall renew their
strength; they shall mount up with wings like eagles, they shall run and
not be weary, they shall walk and not faint."

I am learning, especially in the waiting seasons, that God puts us in
places of waiting to:

- Change us.
- Change the place we are waiting.

You can change the atmosphere and attitudes around you. Be encouraged—you can speak words of life. Proverbs 18:21 (NLT) tells us,
"The tongue can bring death or life." Words give life! Is the atmosphere changed in a positive way because of your presence?

Ephesians 1:18 (ESV) says, "Having the eyes of your hearts enlight-
ened, that you may know what is the hope to which he has called you,
what are the riches of his glorious inheritance in the saints."

From John MacArthur's New Testament commentary:

> The cost of true greatness is humble, selfless, sacrificial ser-
> vice. The Christian who desires to be great and first in the
> kingdom is the one who is willing to serve in the hard place,
> the uncomfortable place, the lonely place, the demanding
> place, the place where he is not appreciated and may even be
> persecuted. Knowing that time is short and eternity long, he
> is willing to spend and be spent. He is willing to work for
> excellence without becoming proud, to withstand criticism
> without becoming bitter, to be misjudged without becoming
> defensive, and to withstand suffering without succumbing to
> self-pity.[13]

---

13   John MacArthur, *Matthew 16–23: The MacArthur New Testament Commentary*
(Moody Publishers, 1988).

Focus Verse

"May the God of hope fill you with all joy and peace as you trust in him, so that you may overflow with hope by the power of the Holy Spirit" (Rom. 15:13).

Connecting the Dots

Let us seize and hold tightly the confession of our hope without wavering, for He who promised is reliable and trustworthy and faithful [to His word]; and let us consider [thoughtfully] how we may encourage one another to love and to do good deeds, not forsaking our meeting together [as believers for worship and instruction], as is the habit of some, but encouraging one another; and all the more [faithfully] as you see the day [of Christ's return] approaching. (Hebrews 10:23–25 AMP)

Make It Personal

Pray Romans 15:13 back to God and ask that it be made real in your life.

_____

_____

I say, "I am Debbie Stuart and I HAVE HOPE!"

Chapter Fourteen

One Woman

"She did what she could."
Mark 14:8

"Many … from that town believed in him because of the woman's testimony."
John 4:39

I have lived long enough to realize that ONE woman, used by God, has the power to change the very course of history. YOU can be a world changer. Today, I want to talk about YOU and the role one woman can play in changing lives. Please allow me a moment to swallow the huge lump I feel climbing up in my throat, as what I am about to share is extremely personal. I am a life that was changed by one woman stepping into the life of one woman.

Her name was Carol. She was my mom. She lost a courageous battle with aggressive cancer when she was forty. I was twenty-three and had a five-week-old baby boy, her first grandchild. She lives in heaven now. The story I am about to share is one she told me as I sat on the side of her hospital bed, about three weeks before she stepped into heaven. This is my rendition of it: When she was sixteen, she married my dad, leaving home and school to escape an unhealthy home life. She soon realized my dad had a raging battle with alcohol.

Shortly thereafter, on a Saturday morning she found herself overwhelmed with hopelessness and despair and had thoughts of suicide. She knew that would not be the right thing to do, so she did what she could to change her situation. It started with planting flowers in her front yard. It was that very morning that Mrs. Jean (a sweet lady next door) saw my mom from her kitchen window, planting flowers … and wiping tears as she did.

Mrs. Jean put down her dish towel and walked across the front yard. She asked my mom if she was okay. My mom replied (like any good Southern woman), "I'm fine!"

Mrs. Jean knew she wasn't fine. She introduced herself and invited my mom to church the next day. My mom replied, "I have tried everything else. I guess I could try religion." But then she said, "I better not. I'm sure women wear dresses at your church, and I don't have a dress." Mrs. Jean told her she could wear pants and that she would wear pants too.

Mom didn't know Mrs. Jean had never worn pants to church. And that afternoon she (Mrs. Jean) called women from the pictorial directory (that was the equivalent of a group text back then) and told them all to wear pants to church the next day.

My mom went to church with her the next day and for the first time, she heard about God's love, how He died on a cross to save her, and how she could have a relationship with Him. She learned she was never meant to live in despair and be hopeless. She was filled with hope. My mom gave her life to Christ that day. The women's group there welcomed her with open arms even though she was "different." The women's class called themselves the "Deborah class." They gave her a Bible, bought her some dresses, and began to teach her God's Word and about God's love. They began to pour into her life. My mom began to thrive, and her life was changed. Not long after that, she became pregnant with me and named me Deborah Jean. After ONE woman who walked across a front yard and invited my mom to church. And after a group of women that loved her and invested in her life. Here comes that lump again.

Then there was me. As a grieving young woman with a five-week-old baby boy, I found myself at a very dark place in life. I didn't understand about postpartum depression and the grief of losing my mom was life-shattering. I missed my mom terribly.

Then one woman stepped into my life. She spoke truth into my life and taught me how to walk with the Lord and how pain can be used for my progress. She recognized and affirmed God's call on my life to ministry and she championed my spiritual growth. So many times I wanted to quit, but she would have none of that. "Not on my watch," she would say.

"Things I Miss"

An easy thing, O Power Divine,
To thank Thee for these gifts of mine.
For summer's sunshine, winter's snow.
For hearts that kindle, thoughts that glow.
But when shall I attain to this:
To thank Thee for the things I miss?

For all young fancy's early gleams,
The dreamed of joys that still are dreams.
Hopes unfulfilled, and pleasures known
Through others fortunes, not my own.
And blessings seen that are not given,
And never will be this side of Heaven.

Had I too shared the joys I see,
Would there have been a plan for me?
Could I have felt Thy presence near
Had I possessed what I held dear?
My deepest fortune, highest bliss,
Have grown, perchance, from the things I miss.

Sometimes there comes an hour of calm,
Grief turns to blessing, pain to balm.
A Power that works above my will
Still leads me on and upward still;
And then my heart shall attain to this:
To thank Thee for the things I miss.

(Author Unknown)

Here comes that lump again.

> *"The Lord is near to the brokenhearted and saves the crushed in spirit"* (Ps. 34:18 ESV).

Now, you don't know me, but I have had the greatest privilege of leading women's ministry for thirty-three years—ten years at one of the largest churches in the United States. You need to know it was not because of skill, education, or any other personal ability. I have committed my lifetime to ministry because years ago one woman stepped into the life of one woman. One woman became involved and invested in one woman. Not only did it change the life of one woman, but it has changed thousands and it has also changed the very course of history.

> *"Many … from that town believed in him because of the woman's testimony"* (John 4:39).

Since then, many women have stepped into the lives of many women and one by one lives have been changed, history has been altered, and the gates of hell have been pushed back just a little.

What life will YOU step into?

Who knows what the Lord has planned for them, with your help.

> *"You shall also be a crown of glory in the hand of the Lord"* (Isa. 62:3 NKJV).

Focus Verse

"She did what she could" (Mark 14:8).

"Many … from that town believed in him because of the woman's testimony"
(John 4:39).

Connecting the Dots

One woman is of priceless value to God's kingdom, and YOU may be that woman!

I hope today you will commit to being used by God, not because you are gifted or qualified, but because God has asked you to.

> This is my life work: helping people understand and respond to this Message. It came as a sheer gift to me, a real surprise, God handling all the details. When it came to presenting the Message to people who had no background in God's way, I was the least qualified of any of the available Christians. God saw to it that I was equipped, but you can be sure that it had nothing to do with my natural abilities. My task is to bring out in the open and make plain what God, who created all this in the first place, has been doing in secret and behind the scenes all along. (Ephesians 3:7–9 MSG)

> "Then Abraham waited patiently, and he received what God had promised" (Heb. 6:15 NLT).

Elizabeth Elliott said, "Don't dig up in doubt what you have planted in faith."

Ephesians 3:14–21 is one of the most powerful and beautiful prayers in the Bible. It's packed with deep spiritual truth and heartfelt requests. This is my prayer for you:

> My response is to get down on my knees before the Father, this magnificent Father who parcels out all heaven and earth. I ask him to strengthen you by his Spirit—not a brute strength but a glorious inner strength—that Christ will live in you as you open the door and invite him in. And I ask him that with both feet planted firmly on love, you'll be able to take in with all followers of Jesus the extravagant dimensions of Christ's love. Reach out and experience the breadth! Test its length! Plumb the depths! Rise to the heights! Live full lives, full in the fullness of God. God can do anything, you know—far more than you could ever imagine or guess or request in your wildest dreams! He does it not by pushing us around but by working

within us, his Spirit deeply and gently within us. (Ephesians 3:14–21 MSG)

Make It Personal

Prayer Points from Ephesians 3:14–21 (ESV):

1. **To be strengthened by God with inner strength**. "That … he may grant you to be strengthened with power through his Spirit in your inner being …" (v. 16). Pray for inner strength through the Holy Spirit to face trials, resist temptation, and grow spiritually.

2. **For Christ to dwell in your heart through faith.** "… so that Christ may dwell in your hearts through faith …" (v. 17). Ask for Jesus to be at home in your heart—not as a guest, but as the ruling and abiding King.

3. **To be rooted and grounded in love.** "… that you, being rooted and grounded in love …" (v. 17). Pray that you would make time with the Lord a priority and grow spiritually, helping others to grow as well.

4. **To comprehend the vastness of Christ's love**. "… may have strength to comprehend … what is the breadth and length and height and depth …" (v. 18). Ask for spiritual understanding to grasp how the Lord is working in your life and through your circumstances.

5. **To know the love of Christ that surpasses knowledge**. "… and to know the love of Christ that surpasses knowledge …" (v. 19). Pray not just to understand Christ's love intellectually, but to experience it personally and deeply.

6. **To be filled with all the fullness of God.** "… that you may be filled with all the fullness of God" (v. 19). Ask for your heart, mind, and life to be filled with God's presence, character, and power.

7. **To trust God's power to do more than you ask or imagine**. "Now to him who is able to do far more abundantly than all that we ask or think ..." (v. 20). Pray with confidence in God's power to work beyond your imagination—in your life, family, church, and world—one life at a time.

From one woman to one woman, with love,

Deborah Jean

Chapter Fifteen

The Battle in My Brain

"Don't copy the behavior and customs of this world,
but let God transform you into a new person by changing the way you think.
Then you will learn to know God's will for you,
which is good and pleasing and perfect."
Romans 12:2 (NLT)

I believe this to be one of the most important messages I have ever written. I feel the weight of the TRUTH I am going to try to deliver! *Lord, help me deliver it with clarity and conviction.*

Drawing on Scripture and medical science, we will discover and implement helpful techniques that will enable us to:

- Change the way we think (YES! You can change your brain!).
- Increase our mental awareness.
- Strengthen our emotional well-being.
- Defeat the enemy of our soul.

Habits, hang-ups, thoughts, and behaviors all comprise our way of thinking, resulting in our way of acting which affects our way of life. Unhealthy thought patterns are easy to develop, and they can be hard to break. What you think about grows. Give that some thought! However, with the power of the Holy Spirit at work in our lives and

God's Word for instruction, we CAN change our mind and thereby change our lives.

Let's look at ten ways we can do that, each one supported by Scripture.

Ten Techniques for Training your Brain:

1. **REFUSE NEGATIVE NARRATIVE**

> *We are human, but we don't wage war as humans do. We use God's mighty weapons, not worldly weapons, to knock down the strongholds of human reasoning and to destroy false arguments. We destroy every proud obstacle that keeps people from knowing God. We capture their rebellious thoughts and teach them to obey Christ. (2 Corinthians 10:3–5 NLT)*

A stronghold can be defined as Satan erecting barriers to keep us from knowing the truth. Our phone, for instance, can become a stronghold if it keeps us from being in God's Word and knowing the truth. (You're welcome for that!) And "God's mighty weapons" are described in ESV and NLT Bibles as:

- God's Word
- Prayer
- Faith
- Hope
- Love
- The power of the Holy Spirit

Many of us have developed a faulty belief system. The enemy is constantly throwing negative thoughts into our mind and creating false narratives. Most often they are straight-up lies. God's Word tell us that Satan is the father of lies and a deceiver. Here are some characteristics and strategies of the enemy from Scripture:

- The devil has a plan, a purpose, and a will for your life (see John 10:10).
- He is like a roaring lion seeking someone to devour (see 1 Peter 5:8).

- He disguises himself as an angel of light (see 2 Corinthians 11:14).
- He is a destroyer. His purpose is to destroy God's work, plan, and purposes (see John 8:44).
- The Bible describes him as the adversary, the enemy, and the accuser (see Luke 10:19).
- He is a deceiver (see Revelation 20:7–8).
- He is the father of lies (see John 8:44).

In Craig Groeschel's book *Winning the War in Your Mind*, he states that "our minds are always moving in the direction of our strongest thoughts."[14] As stated by many authors in the past, our minds are a battlefield! To defeat the enemy on this battlefield we must engage with truth and refuse negative, unhealthy narratives the enemy seeks to plant in this battlefield.

There is a general scientific consensus that people think around six thousand thoughts per day. Now, for an overthinker like me—I am sure I am running upwards of ten thousand! A study by *Psychology Today* entitled "Wicked Thoughts" reveals that we are bombarded by about five hundred unintentional, negative, and intrusive thoughts a day.[15] Each unwanted thought lasts about fourteen seconds. Do the math. That's almost two hours a day of thoughts we do not want to think. Then multiply that with issues you have to think about such as financial issues, health issues, marriage, children, physical things, work things, relationships, and so much more.

Those "wicked thoughts" or unwanted thoughts have been referred to as **ANTS: Automatic Negative Thoughts.** They are cynical, negative, gloomy, or complaining thoughts that seem to multiply and come to mind unsolicited. Left uncontrolled or allowed, they have been known to break down your immune system and nervous system causing an onslaught of physical illnesses.

---

14   Craig Groeschel, *Winning the War in Your Mind: Change Your Thinking, Change Your Life* (Zondervan, 2021).

15   Jena E. Pincott, "Wicked Thoughts," Psychology Today, September 1, 2015, https://www.psychologytoday.com/us/articles/201509/wicked-thoughts.

You must think about what you think about!

What you feed your mind and the thoughts you think influence your mental and emotional wellbeing. The Lord tells us, "For my thoughts are not your thoughts, neither are your ways my ways, declares the LORD" (Isa. 55:8–9 ESV).

He says in 1 Peter 5:8 (ESV), "Be sober-minded; be watchful. Your adversary the devil prowls around like a roaring lion, seeking someone to devour." And his game is mental! The enemy throws anything and everything he can at your mind and sees what will stick to get your brain to react in a way that is destructive to you. When he gets your attention with some harmful, intrusive thought, he will wear you out with it. **His weapon is a lie, and his strategy is repetition.** Because he knows once you think it, it will be easier to get you to think it again … so it grows.

For example, our son, Jarrad, struggled with an addiction for many years and served time in prison. We have talked through his journey and how it all happened many times. Here's how it started. He believed a lie. The enemy put a thought in his mind that we were trying to control his life. The enemy repeated that lie that we were trying to take his freedom. Over and over, he heard words like: "You can be free! You don't have to follow their stupid rules. This is your life. Do what you want! Be free of them. They are trying to tell you what to do and run your life. You don't have to do it. Be free! Leave! Do what you want to do. Drugs aren't hurting you; they are helping you cope." And it got easier and easier for him to do more and more drugs, leave home, and claim his "life of freedom." Those choices cost him every ounce of freedom known to man.

No doubt the devil thought it was all a very successful attempt at taking his life. And it almost took me down as well. "But as for you, you meant evil against me; but God meant it for good" (Gen. 50:20 NKJV).

Have you ever heard people say things like:

- You can't swim for thirty minutes after you eat.
- Cracking your knuckles will cause arthritis.

- Shaving makes your hair grow back thicker.

Do you know why we believed these things? We believed it because it was repeated … for generations! We believed it because it was repeated NOT because it was true. None of those things are true. There is absolutely no reason medically why you can't swim after you eat. It does not cause cramps. Many of us have wasted countless moments sitting on the shore, waiting for thirty minutes to go by.

Our brain is constantly evolving. Neurologists call the process neuroplasticity. The idea is that we can build our brain like we build our muscles with some strategic time spent in the gym. Your brain is re-wiring itself all the time by creating new neural pathways. It has the ability to renew and restore damaged area.

2. **REMOVE TOXIC THOUGHTS**

> *Those who are dominated by the sinful nature think about sinful things, but those who are controlled by the Holy Spirit think about things that please the Spirit. So letting your sinful nature control your mind leads to death. But letting the Spirit control your mind leads to life and peace. (Romans 8:5–6 NLT)*

I've tried to talk the Lord out of sharing this personal illustration, but I was unsuccessful. So here goes. Almost every time after I teach a message or a Bible study lesson, before I can get to my car or back to my office, a thought hits me, pretty hard.

It goes something like this:

- That was the stupidest thing you have ever shared.
- None of that made any sense—you rambled on and on.
- Now people just feel sorry for you.
- You should really STOP DOING THIS!

Before I can catch a breath to rebuke the enemy, he has bombarded me with repetitive, negative thoughts that are intended to "get me to thinking," to hurt me, and to stop me.

How do I remove those toxic thoughts? I worship!

One of my favorite songs to belt out in those moments of degrading thoughts is:

"I Raise a Hallelujah" by Bethel Music. Pull it up on YouTube. Some of the lyrics include:

> *I raise a hallelujah*
> *In the presence of my enemies*
> *I raise a hallelujah*
> *Louder than the unbelief*
>
> *I raise a hallelujah*
> *My weapon is a melody*
> *I raise a hallelujah*
> *Heaven comes to fight for me*
>
> *I'm gonna sing*
> *In the middle of the storm*
> *Louder and louder*
> *You're gonna hear my praises roar*
> *Up from the ashes, hope will arise*
> *Death is defeated, the King is alive![16]*

When toxic thoughts are not dealt with and destroyed, they tend to destroy us. Remember, Satan is the destroyer. Those thoughts can grow into forms and levels of depression, anxiety, panic, worry, stress, shame, and fear. All of which have been proven to have a negative impact on our physical body.

3. **REMEMBER, THINK QUICK!**

"Stay alert! Watch out for your great enemy, the devil. He prowls around like a roaring lion, looking for someone to devour. Stand firm against him, and be strong in your faith" (1 Pet. 5:8–9 NLT).

Learn to "catch a thought"! Think about what you think about! As soon as the negative thought comes in, say, "NO! I am not going to

---

16   Jonathan David Helser and Melissa Helser, "Raise a Hallelujah," *Victory*, Bethel Music Publishing, 2019.

think that way." You can bind that thought or that thought can bind you. How do you bind a thought? You take it captive.

> *The weapons we fight with are not the weapons of the world. On the contrary, they have divine power to demolish strongholds. We demolish arguments and every pretension that sets itself up against the knowledge of God, and we take captive every thought to make it obedient to Christ. (2 Corinthians 10:4–5)*

You're going to need to learn some truth. Think for minute and be honest with yourself. How many Bible verses do you know by heart? Can you grab some quickly? A Bible app will help. One process that helps me a great deal is to write Scriptures on index cards. I have hundreds by this point. I keep them in little index card binders. I keep them close on my bathroom mirror, in the

Learn to "catch a thought"!

kitchen, in my car, in my purse. Here's a thought: Next time you stop at a red light, don't pick up your phone—pick up your index cards and read and recite Scripture.

Crazy and random thoughts will hijack your emotions, your attitude, and your decisions. Think about what you think about.

4. **RENEW YOUR MIND**

> *Therefore, I urge you, brothers and sisters, in view of God's mercy, to offer your bodies as a living sacrifice, holy and pleasing to God—this is your true and proper worship. Do not conform to the pattern of this world, but be transformed by the renewing of your mind. Then you will be able to test and approve what God's will is—his good, pleasing and perfect will. (Romans 12:1–2)*

This passage deserves some personal study time. It instructs us on how to renew our mind, which is a foundational principle in transformation and spiritual growth. Renewing your mind involves replacing lies with God's truth. A renewed mind enables you to recognize and align with God's activity and His will.

Renewing your mind can be done from a recliner, lying in bed, driving a car, sitting on a porch swing, walking—anytime!

Prayer changes your brain!

5. **REPLACE WITH TRUTH**

> *So humble yourselves before God. Resist the devil, and he will flee from you. Come close to God, and God will come close to you. Wash your hands, you sinners; purify your hearts, for your loyalty is divided between God and the world. (James 4:7–8 NLT)*

The Message Bible translation of these verses says:

> *So let God work his will in you. Yell a loud no to the Devil and watch him make himself scarce. Say a quiet yes to God and he'll be there in no time. Quit dabbling in sin. Purify your inner life. Quit playing the field. Hit bottom and cry your eyes out. The fun and games are over. Get serious, really serious. Get down on your knees before the Master; it's the only way you'll get on your feet.*

A great example of this in the Bible is found in 2 Kings 5. It is the story of Naaman. I hope you will take some time to read it. Naaman had leprosy. He appealed to Elisha for healing. (There is more to it than that! Naaman had a hard time with instructions, feelings, and his thought processes.)

When Elisha did not heal Naaman the way he thought he should, the Bible says, "But Naaman became angry and stalked away. 'I thought he would certainly come out to meet me!' he said. 'I expected him to wave his hand over the leprosy and call on the name of the LORD his God and heal me!'" (2 Kings 5:11 NLT).

Naaman stalked away in a rage. Why? He received instructions for how to be healed, so why was he so mad? Because it did not happen the way he "thought" and he "expected."

He almost forfeited his healing because of his thinking!

Some of us are asking the Lord to arrange certain things or change things in our lives, but we won't arrange things or change things.

When nothing changes … nothing changes!

Focus Verse

"Don't copy the behavior and customs of this world, but let God transform you into a new person by changing the way you think. Then you will learn to know God's will for you, which is good and pleasing and perfect" (Rom. 12:2 NLT).

Connecting the Dots

Knowing God's will for our lives is critical for changing our thinking. It is not as difficult as we may think. We know God's will as we surrender our hearts and minds to Him. As we do, we develop a passion for reading and understanding His Word, accepting His love, and having a personal relationship with Jesus Christ. We are changed—transformed in the way we live, think, and respond to others. His will is for us to be with Him forever, and that is made possible by our commitment, surrender, and relationship with Jesus.

Make It Personal

Do your thoughts reflect gentleness, kindness, thankfulness, faith, hope, and joy? Do they point you to do good, think good about people, and look for ways to serve and speak gently and positively to them?

_____

_____

Do your thoughts reflect negativity, worry, stress, insecurity, anxiety, negativity, suspicion, and exhaustion—overwhelming you and leaving you feeling helpless and hopeless?

_____

_____

Whether you think you can or think you can't ... either way, you're right.

NOTE: The remaining five techniques for training your brain are continued in chapter sixteen.

The Battle in My Brain (continued)

"You keep him in perfect peace
whose mind is stayed on you,
because he trusts in you."
Isaiah 26:3 (ESV)

Let's continue to work through what God's Word teaches about our mind, our thoughts, and the processes and actions that are set in motion through those two avenues.

Often, I have prayed and asked the Lord to take away my anxiety or help me walk through it. What I have learned from the Lord is: "Let's work on and walk through the *cause* of your anxiety." I pray that through this chapter you sense the voice of the Lord directing your next steps.

It's not so important what happened to you, or what you did—what's more important is what you do next.

Ten Techniques for Training your Brain (continued):

6. **RETRAIN YOUR BRAIN**

"The thief's purpose is to steal and kill and destroy. My purpose is to give them a rich and satisfying life" (John 10:10 NLT).

Retraining your brain is about aligning your thoughts with God's truth rather than the world's customs. It is about reframing situations, conversations, and thought processes. When a thought comes in, ask: "Is this true?"

Ask the Holy Spirit to expose wrong thought patterns and faulty belief systems, and to empower you to think thoughts that are in accordance with God's Word and God's will.

> ## Ask the Holy Spirit to expose wrong thought patterns and faulty belief systems.

Fill your mind with God's Word "Your word is a lamp to my feet and a light to my path" (Ps. 119:105 NKJV).

Let me give you two examples from my own life to hopefully demonstrate a retraining process.

First: My doctor indicated that I should use weights for my arms, to reshape them and give me strength. All of which I wanted and needed. I knew it would be entirely beneficial. However, here's what I thought every time I passed by the weights on my table: "I hate those weights!" And I would talk myself out of using them. I got it in my mind that it was hard, and I didn't like it. So, I didn't do it.

To retrain my brain, I started thinking differently. When I walked by the weights I thought: "These are very helpful. I'm very thankful I have the ability to get stronger. I love how I feel and how my arms look." This caused my brain to react differently when I saw the weights.

Second: We live on a lake with a big backyard. For a couple of years, I walked down to the water through the middle of my backyard. Guess what it created? Correct, it created a pathway. A hard pathway where no grass grew. My sweet husband asked me one day, "Could you please walk down on the side of the yard by the fence?"

I started doing that and guess what happened? Growth happened and the bare path changed to its intended purpose. Grass grew and the path went away.

You have the ability to create change!

7. **REFRAME YOUR THOUGHTS**

> *"And I want you to know, my dear brothers and sisters, that everything that has happened to me here has helped to spread the Good News" (Phil. 1:12 NLT).*

Reframing your thoughts is what medical professionals in the psychotherapeutic world call *cognitive reframing*. It's when we learn to IDENTIFY and CORRECT irrational and stress-driven thinking.

Our frame is how we view things (FILTER) and how we interpret what's happening. To reframe something means we look at it differently and choose a more productive and healthy perspective and mindset of the circumstances.

For instance, a friend of mine had a car wreck, totaled her car, went to the hospital, and was waiting on results from an X-ray. I was with her and saw this process take place. She starting thinking negative thoughts. (Side note: Don't even start thinking that way!)

Then she started saying, "This is the worst thing ever! This is the worst timing! This is so not good!" She became more and more upset, frustrated, and mad. Her blood pressure started going up. Her heartrate started going up. All the negative emotional things ramped up some negative physical things which caused a medical problem.

When the X-rays came back, there were no broken bones, but it revealed a mass in her chest area. It was a slow-growing tumor that often turns cancerous. The doctors said without that X-ray AT THAT TIME it very likely would have developed into cancer. So, before we get all bent out of shape because **we think** something is bad, remember that the Lord is working ALL things out for our good to those who love God and are called according to His purpose!

Here are some steps to help us reframe our thoughts:

- **Stay calm.** Don't overact to situations; don't overthink it and blow it out of proportion.
- **Get perspective**.
- **Identify steps to fix the problem.**

A biblical example is Paul: "And I want you to know, my dear brothers and sisters, that everything that has happened to me here has helped to spread the Good News" (Phil. 1:12 NLT).

We cannot control what happens to us, but we CAN CONTROL how we frame it.

8. **PRE-FRAME YOUR FUTURE**

"And God is able to bless you abundantly, so that in all things at all times, having all that you need, you will abound in every good work" (2 Cor. 9:8 NIV).

Pre-framing is choosing how I will view something BEFORE it happens.

We can decide right now to trust the Lord. We can decide that in a crisis we will wait on the Lord so we can renew our strength.

Read 1 Thessalonians 5:16–18.

- Always be joyful (see verse 16).
- Keep on praying (see verse 17).
- No matter what happens, always be thankful, for this is God's will for you (see verse 18).

This is so helpful to us especially when there is trauma, emotional distress, anxiety, or physical pain. These emotions and experiences have the ability to change the chemistry in our brain.

Every night we should pre-frame the next day—get our mind thinking in the right direction. Instead of going to bed and thinking, "Tomorrow is going to be a busy/hard day and I'm dreading it. I dread this meeting or conversation or doctor's visit or exercise program. I dread driving. I don't want to change diapers"—instead of repeating the things we won't like about tomorrow—pre-frame it! Be thankful. Look at the blessings and the benefits. Pray.

Lord, I trust You for tomorrow, knowing You will guide me through the day, even the hard things I don't want to do. Fill my heart with joy for the opportunity to serve my family and others. Amen.

Dread creates apprehension with the assumption that something will not be good. It causes fear, worry, anxiety, and an overwhelming sense of dissatisfaction. Hope is the opposite. It is the expectation of something good. We need to begin our days with hope, not dread.

Instead of complaining how hard it will be, how bad it will be, or how much we don't like it or don't want to do it, pre-framing will retrain our brain in a new way of responding and forecasting. Then, when the unexpected comes and it is out of our control, we already have a PRESET mindset, attitude, perspective, and belief system that will stabilize and anchor us in times of storms.

Don't forecast the worst possible outcome.

Instead, anchor in God's Word.

9. **REJOICE MINDSET**

Rejoice in the Lord always. I will say it again: Rejoice! Let your gentleness be evident to all. The Lord is near. Do not be anxious about anything, but in every situation, by prayer and petition, with thanksgiving, present your requests to God. And the peace of God, which transcends all understanding, will guard your hearts and your minds in Christ Jesus. (Philippians 4:4–7).

"Set your minds on things above, not on earthly things" (Col. 3:2).

10. **RESOLVE MENTALITY**

"Finally, be strong in the Lord and in his mighty power. Put on the full armor of God, so that you can take your stand against the devil's schemes" (Eph. 6:10–11).

Our mind is a battlefield and spiritual warfare is real. You need equipment and God has provided it. Your strength comes from God. You must be spiritually alert and ready.

In his book *Winning the War in Your Mind,* Craig Groeschel recommends a "God box."[17] It's a box (any size you desire) intended to serve as a visual reminder to take our thoughts to God. He explains that every time we have a worry, burden, temptation, runaway thought, or critical/negative attitude, we should write it on a slip of paper and put it in our God box. That represents YOU giving that burden/stress/thought to the Lord. Then pray: *God, I am trusting You with this and I know You are in control of it. This is not a thought I want to think so I am giving it to You to hold captive.*

Some of us are asking God to help us see His plan, but we don't stop looking at social media long enough to see it.

Fight back with **spiritual weapons** and **spiritual vengeance**!

You are NOT powerless against the schemes of the enemy! Take back what the enemy has stolen from you.

In closing, what do you sense from the Lord? What is He stirring in you and saying to you at this moment?

"Finally, be strengthened by the Lord and by his vast strength" (Eph. 6:10 CSB).

In *The Message* Bible, Ephesians 6:10–12 says:

A Fight to the Finish

And that about wraps it up. God is strong, and he wants you strong. So take everything the Master has set out for you, well-made weapons of the best materials. And put them to use so you will be able to stand up to everything the Devil throws your way. This is no weekend war that we'll walk away from and forget about in a couple of hours. This is for keeps, a life-or-death fight to the finish against the Devil and all his angels.

17　　Craig Groeschel, *Winning the War in Your Mind: Change Your Thinking, Change Your Life* (Zondervan, 2021).

Focus Verse

"You keep him in perfect peace whose mind is stayed on you, because he trusts in you"
(Isa. 26:3 ESV).

Connecting the Dots

How do we have perfect peace? By keeping our mind on God and trusting Him. The ten techniques for training our brain are listed in review below. These are written in a way that we can easily refer to them when our mind goes astray.

The Battle in My Brain! Ten Techniques for Training Your Brain:

1. **REFUSE NEGATIVE NARRATIVE**
   "We are human, but we don't wage war as humans do. We use God's mighty weapons, not worldly weapons, to knock down the strongholds of human reasoning and to destroy false arguments. We destroy every proud obstacle that keeps people from knowing God. We capture their rebellious thoughts and teach them to obey Christ" (2 Cor. 10:3–5 NLT).

2. **REMOVE TOXIC THOUGHTS**
   "Those who are dominated by the sinful nature think about sinful things, but those who are controlled by the Holy Spirit think about things that please the Spirit. So letting your sinful nature control your mind leads to death. But letting the Spirit control your mind leads to life and peace" (Rom. 8:5–6 NLT).

3. **REMEMBER - THINK QUICK!**
   "Stay alert! Watch out for your great enemy, the devil. He prowls around like a roaring lion, looking for someone to devour. Stand firm against him, and be strong in your faith" (1 Pet. 5:8–9 NLT).

4. **RENEW YOUR MIND**

   "Therefore, I urge you, brothers and sisters, in view of God's mercy, to offer your bodies as a living sacrifice, holy and pleasing to God—this is your true and proper worship. Do not conform to the pattern of this world, but be transformed by the renewing of your mind. Then you will be able to test and approve what God's will is—his good, pleasing and perfect will" (Rom. 12:1–2).

5. **REPLACE WITH TRUTH**

   "So humble yourselves before God. Resist the devil, and he will flee from you. Come close to God, and God will come close to you. Wash your hands, you sinners; purify your hearts, for your loyalty is divided between God and the world" (Jas. 4:7–8 NLT).

   "So let God work his will in you. Yell a loud no to the Devil and watch him make himself scarce. Say a quiet yes to God and he'll be there in no time. Quit dabbling in sin. Purify your inner life. Quit playing the field. Hit bottom and cry your eyes out. The fun and games are over. Get serious, really serious. Get down on your knees before the Master; it's the only way you'll get on your feet" (Jas. 4:7–8 MSG).

6. **RETRAIN YOUR BRAIN**

   "The thief's purpose is to steal and kill and destroy. My purpose is to give them a rich and satisfying life" (John 10:10 NLT).

7. **REFRAME YOUR THOUGHTS**

   "And I want you to know, my dear brothers and sisters, that everything that has happened to me here has helped to spread the Good News" (Phil. 1:12 NLT).

8. **PRE-FRAME YOUR FUTURE**

   "And God is able to bless you abundantly, so that in all things at all times, having all that you need, you will abound in every good work" (2 Cor. 9:8).

9. **REJOICE MINDSET**

   "Rejoice in the Lord always. I will say it again: Rejoice! Let your gentleness be evident to all. The Lord is near. Do not be anxious about anything, but in every situation, by prayer and petition, with thanksgiving,

present your requests to God. And the peace of God, which transcends all understanding, will guard your hearts and your minds in Christ Jesus" (Phil. 4:4–7).

"Set your minds on things above, not on earthly things" (Col. 3:2).

10. **RESOLVE MENTALITY**
"Finally, be strong in the Lord and in his mighty power. Put on the full armor of God, so that you can take your stand against the devil's schemes" (Eph. 6:10–11).

Make It Personal

The following is a list of good thoughts versus toxic thoughts. First, read through the toxic thoughts. Then ask the Lord to remove any of them that trip you up. Place a large *X* over all the thoughts that you struggle with.

Next, look up each Scripture in the **Helpful Thoughts and Big Truth** list. There are three things to see as you read them. In the blank space in front of the reference, place either a *P, A,* or *C.*

- **P**romise – God's promises to remember for hope and encouragement.
- **A**ction – Instruction to practice daily.
- **C**laim – Statements we can claim and live by.

PAC these in your heart, mind, and prayers for a renewed sense of peace and way of thinking.

Then as you read the **ANTS** to look out for, draw a circle over them and write the word *STOP* in the circle as your commitment to hold your thoughts captive to God.

Think This ... Not That!

"For as he thinks in his heart, so is he" (Prov. 23:7 NKJV).

Toxic Thoughts & Little Lies	**Helpful Thoughts & Big Truth**
1. This is not good.	1. _P_ Psalm 22:24
	(Example: Promise)
2. This is too hard.	2. __Psalm 94:18
3. I can't do this anymore.	3. __Psalm 147:3
4. God doesn't care about me.	4. __Romans 8:28; John 11:35
5. I can't help the way I am.	5. __Matthew 16:24–26
6. This will never change.	6. __Lamentations 3:22–23
7. This is a waste of time.	7. __1 Corinthians 15:58
8. This is the worst thing ever!	8. __Job 23:10
9. I am stupid and worthless.	9. __2 Corinthians 12:10
10. I don't want to live.	10. __Philippians 3:14; Romans 10:13
11. This habit isn't really that bad.	11. __Hebrews 12:1–2
12. Nobody cares about me.	12. __Matthew 10:30–31
13. I will never be happy.	13. __Psalm 30:5
14. I can't help the way I feel.	14. __Philippians 4:8
15. I will never be able to get over this.	15. __Psalm 23:4
16. I just can't take this anymore.	16. __John 16:33
17. There is no point in trying to fix this.	17. __Isaiah 57:18–19
18. This is going to be a terrible day.	18. __Psalm 118:24
19. Everybody else has a good life.	19. __Galatians 1:10
20. I hate the way things are right now.	20. __Nahum 1:7
21. No one knows what I'm going through.	21. __Psalm 139; Hebrews 4:16
I am so tired, exhausted, and weary.	22. __Hebrews 12:3
22. God isn't doing anything.	23. __Hebrews 10:23; Jude 22
23. What will my friends think?	24. __Psalm 25:1–3
24. I am losing my (ever-lovin') mind!	25. __Mark 5:36

Watch Out for ANTS: Automatic Negative Thoughts

- I am the victim here!
- Nobody wants to be my friend.
- No one ever talks to me.
- Everybody thinks I am an idiot.
- This always happens to me!
- My past will determine my future.
- The grass is greener on the other side.
- This is making me sick. *(If you keep thinking that—it will!)*
- I am so tired.
- I am so hurt.
- I am so mad.

Chapter Seventeen

A Lifetime of Purpose and Productivity

*"Let your roots grow down into him, and let your lives be built on him.
Then your faith will grow strong in the truth you were taught,
and you will overflow with thankfulness."*
Colossians 2:7 (NLT)

I have the heart of a gardener; I guess it serves my need to nurture something. I love to watch something grow and especially love it when a plant grows big and beautiful after a long, hard winter. Many times in the Bible God illustrates His message about developing Christlike attributes and growing in spiritual maturity by using an analogy of a garden, a tree, or a field. Overall, the Bible encourages believers to pursue spiritual growth, continually deepening our understanding of God's Word. We are instructed to be rooted, established, strengthened, and thankful, all of which will cultivate a life that produces much fruit.

One of our grandsons, Gunner, was born six weeks early. The doctors were concerned with his weight and growth. After a couple of weeks, measurement indicated he was not growing. It was said that he had a "failure to thrive." Then the doctor said, "We must investigate this immediately. We must determine WHY he is not growing and fix that problem." If you aren't growing, there is a problem that needs to be identified and fixed. Growth shows!

I hope this chapter is like pouring Miracle-Gro all over your life. Through God's Word we are going to discuss some gardening illustrations, but we will look at all of those from a spiritual growth filter. I am praying this will be personally enriching, spiritually beneficial, and very meaningful in your life.

The Bible teaches us that God wants us to grow spiritually. Our lives are to produce good things, good fruit, and the fruit of the Spirit. God prunes our lives to produce MORE good things. His Word goes on to say not just MORE, but MUCH fruit!

In cultivating plants and gardens, I have learned this important fact: What you do or do not do in February and March affects what will or will not happen in April and May. It's not so much what has happened—it's what happens next that is so important.

> **It's not so much what has happened—it's what happens next that is so important.**

When our neighbor plants his garden every spring, he does not walk to the garden area and start throwing seeds on the ground. What does he do first? He prepares the soil. He takes some things out (grass, weeds, rocks). He puts some things in (fertilizer, cow manure, compost).

Why? Because when the conditions are right, things will grow! The same is true for our lives.

The conditions are on us to **PREPARE**! Conditions are choices you make.

To cultivate means to prepare to acquire, to grow, and to improve through labor, care, or study. As you cultivate the soil of your life, what are some things that need to come out? What needs to be added? One thing I have added to my life to promote spiritual growth is spending time with the Lord in His Word every day.

Growth challenge: Twenty Minutes a Day for the Rest of Your Life.

Time with the Lord every day will build strong faith, a resilient life, and create something big and beautiful even after a long, hard winter season. God promises to lead, satisfy, and strengthen you.

Let's look at what God's Word says about the conditions of our lives. It's been called the Parable of the Sower, and it's found in Mark chapter 4. Parables are stories that tell biblical principles and show personal application.

> *Listen! A farmer went out to plant some seed. As he scattered it across his field, some of the seed fell on a footpath, and the birds came and ate it. Other seed fell on shallow soil with underlying rock. The seed sprouted quickly because the soil was shallow. But the plant soon wilted under the hot sun, and since it didn't have deep roots, it died. Other seed fell among thorns that grew up and choked out the tender plants so they produced no grain. Still other seeds fell on fertile soil, and they sprouted, grew, and produced a crop that was thirty, sixty, and even a hundred times as much as had been planted! (Mark 4:3–8 NLT)*

Let's identify some important components:

- The Sower = The one who shares
- The Seed = The Word of God
- The Soil = The conditions of our life and heart (our mind plays a big part as well)

Then Jesus explains the parable in verses 14–20:

> *The farmer plants seed by taking God's word to others. The seed that fell on the footpath represents those who hear the message, only to have Satan come at once and take it away. The seed on the rocky soil represents those who hear the message and immediately receive it with joy. But since they don't have deep roots, they don't last long. They fall away as soon as they have problems or are persecuted for believing God's word. The seed that fell among the thorns represents others who hear God's word, but all too quickly the message is crowded out by the worries of this life, the lure of*

wealth, and the desire for other things, so no fruit is produced. And the seed that fell on good soil represents those who hear and accept God's word and produce a harvest of thirty, sixty, or even a hundred times as much as had been planted!

This story describes four types of soil:

1. Hard Paths

- People hear but don't believe. They are unwilling to receive the truth.
- The seed produces NOTHING.
- There is *no desire*.

2. Rocky Places

- People hear, but they don't grow.
- They never get around to doing anything about what they heard.
- There is *no difference*.

3. Thorny Patches

- People hear but don't prioritize God's Word.
- Other things are more important. They are distracted, lazy, and discontent.
- Jesus tells us three things that crowd out His Word. These are opponents and obstacles of good soil in our hearts: worries of this life, the lure of wealth, and the desire for other things (cares of this life).
- There is *no room*. Make room for God to work in your life!

A personal faith journey may begin with joy, but when trouble or hardship arise or suffering happens, they give up. There is no depth. Don't waste a crisis! Let it serve the purpose of God.

4. Good Soil

- People hear and hold fast to God's Word. And there is a huge harvest.

- They trust the Lord and follow the Lord wherever, whenever, and whatever.
- There are *no regrets*!

Since the seed is the Word of God, the success or failure of the plant is determined by the soil. If something is not growing, it is not the fault of the seed.

John 15 calls us to bear much fruit. Three out of four did not produce anything. Only one of the seeds produced something.

Don't dig up in unbelief what you have sown in faith.

At present, which soil best represents you and your life? What will you do this week to improve the condition of your "soil"? What needs to go? What needs to be added? Will you make a conscious effort to sow seed this week?

> *"So get rid of all the filth and evil in your lives, and humbly accept the word God has planted in your hearts, for it has the power to save your souls" (Jas. 1:21 NLT).*

> *"The Lord will always lead you, satisfy you in a parched land, and strengthen your bones. You will be like a watered garden and like a spring whose water never runs dry" (Isa. 58:11 CSB).*

> *"And I will give you a new heart, and I will put a new spirit in you. I will take out your* **stony, stubborn heart** *and give you a* **tender, responsive heart***" (Ezek. 36:26 NLT, emphasis mine).*

Lessons from my Greenhouse

- When the conditions are right, things will grow. You are in charge of conditions.
- Big things don't grow in shallow soil.
- Bad stuff grows automatically; good stuff has to be cultivated! Weeds grow naturally as well as vines and fungus, but squash, tomatoes, and good fruit grow when cultivated.
- Poison ivy, weeds, Virginia creeper—I never planted any of those things. They just show up.

Caution: No wonder God insists that we "keep a sharp eye out for weeds of bitter discontent. A thistle or two gone to seed can ruin a whole garden in no time" (Heb. 12:15 MSG).

The cares of the world choke out the Word, and we become unfruitful.

What we do today will have results on what is growing in our life tomorrow.

Read John 15:1–10 (NLT):

> *I am the true grapevine, and my Father is the gardener. He cuts off every branch of mine that doesn't produce fruit, and he prunes the branches that do bear fruit so they will produce even more. You have already been pruned and purified by the message I have given you. Remain in me, and I will remain in you. For a branch cannot produce fruit if it is severed from the vine, and you cannot be fruitful unless you remain in me. Yes, I am the vine; you are the branches. Those who remain in me, and I in them, will produce much fruit. For apart from me you can do nothing. Anyone who does not remain in me is thrown away like a useless branch and withers. Such branches are gathered into a pile to be burned. But if you remain in me and my words remain in you, you may ask for anything you want, and it will be granted! When you produce much fruit, you are my true disciples. This brings great glory to my Father. I have loved you even as the Father has loved me. Remain in my love. When you obey my commandments, you remain in my love, just as I obey my Father's commandments and remain in his love.*

Two things that will make your joy full: ABIDE and REMAIN.

1. **Abide**: Continue to be present. Dwell. Create a constant connection.
2. **Remain**: Endure, persevere, and do not leave.

The enemy wants us to be busy, with no time to spend in Bible study and prayer. This makes us unproductive in the things of God. We become weak, wimpy, whining, and complaining. The enemy wants us to focus on OTHER things and OUR things which are WEEDS, WEEDS, WEEDS!

This passage highlights two more important words: **CUT OFF** and **CUT BACK.**

So, I guess you could say: You are pruned if you do and pruned if you don't!

Think of gardening: Why do gardeners prune trees, bushes, roses, branches, and shrubs?

Ten Reasons for Pruning:

1. **Growth:** Dead branches hinder the growth of healthy branches.
2. **Health**: Prevention and treatment of disease, bugs, and dead limbs.
3. **Production**: Stimulates growth and encourages fruit production, new foliage, and a deeper root system.
4. **Improvement**: Quality and quantity. Dead branches and overgrowth pose a huge risk.
5. **Change**: Shape or train the growth towards a certain direction or pattern.
6. **Control**: Prevents outgrowing and moving into other areas.
7. **Perspective**: Allows you to better see your surroundings. (We cut back trees to see the lake.)
8. **Enlighten**: Let in more light, so more things can grow.
9. **Safety**: Cut tree branches away from power lines, roadways, and cars to minimize damage.
10. **Appearance**: It is pleasing, beautiful, and enjoyable to behold.

The pruning process is necessary and beneficial!

My second to oldest grandson is Luke. One afternoon we were playing outside, and he wasn't having a good day. Things were making him mad, and they weren't going his way. I said to him, "Luke, don't get a bad attitude." To which he responded, "I don't have a bad attitude. It's just my feelings making me fussy." Oh, that is exactly how I feel some days!

"Oh, that my actions would **consistently** *reflect your decrees!" (Ps. 119:5 NLT, emphasis mine).*

Read 2 Peter 1:5–9 (NLT) below. In my Bible, I have a heading that reads: "Need for Faithful Growth in Christ."

In view of all this, make every effort to respond to God's promises. Supplement your faith with a generous provision of moral excellence, and moral excellence with knowledge, and knowledge with self-control, and self-control with patient endurance, and patient endurance with godliness, and godliness with brotherly affection, and brotherly affection with love for everyone. The more you grow like this, the more productive and useful you will be in your knowledge of our Lord Jesus Christ. But those who fail to develop in this way are shortsighted or blind, forgetting that they have been cleansed from their old sins.

These are foundational principles for spiritual growth. We need to keep them ever before us and practice them. Look closely and you will see **seven habits of highly productive believers**:

1. Moral excellence
2. Knowledge of God
3. Self-control
4. Patient endurance
5. Godliness
6. Brotherly affection
7. Love

Caution: "But those who fail to develop in this way are shortsighted or blind" (2 Pet. 1:9 NLT). In verse 8 in another translation (NIV), it says "unproductive." We do not want to be blind, short-sighted, and unproductive in our lives. We want to practice the daily discipline of spending time with God in Bible study and prayer.

You are not getting what you should be getting because you are not sitting where you should be sitting!

Focus Verse

"Let your roots grow down into him, and let your lives be built on him. Then your faith will grow strong in the truth you were taught, and you will overflow with thankfulness" *(Col. 2:7 NLT).*

Connecting the Dots

While preparing this message, I came across a writing by Elizabeth George that was extremely helpful. In her book *A Woman After God's Own Heart*, she talks about the aspects of our "spiritual root system" and how we need a strong, healthy root system produced by the faithful study of God's Word:

> *Roots are unseen*—You'll want to set aside time in solitude—"underground" if you will—to immerse yourself in God's Word and grow in Him.
>
> *Roots are for taking in*—Alone and with your Bible in hand, you'll want to take in and feed upon the truths of the Word of God and ensure your spiritual growth.
>
> *Roots are for storage*—As you form the habit of looking into God's Word, you'll find a vast, deep reservoir of divine hope and strength forming for the rough times.
>
> *Roots are for support*—Do you want to stand strong in the Lord? To stand firm against the pressures of life? The routine care of your roots through exposure to God's Word will cultivate you into a remarkable woman of endurance.[18]
>
> *"They weep as they go to plant their seed, but they sing as they return with the harvest" (Ps. 126:6 NLT).*

---

18   Elizabeth George, *A Woman After God's Own Heart* (Harvest House Publishers, 2015).

Make It Personal

> *Even though the fig trees have no blossoms, and there are no grapes on the vines; even though the olive crop fails, and the fields lie empty and barren; even though the flocks die in the fields, and the cattle barns are empty, yet I will rejoice in the Lord! I will be joyful in the God of my salvation! The Sovereign Lord is my strength! He makes me as surefooted as a deer, able to tread upon the heights. (Habakkuk 3:17–19 NLT)*

In what ways do you relate to Habakkuk or his circumstances?

_____

_____

_____

_____

What choices did he make? What words best describe his mindset?

_____

_____

_____

What can we learn from these Scriptures?

_____

_____

_____

_____

> *"They sow their fields, plant their vineyards, and harvest their bumper crops" (Ps. 107:37 NLT).*

I pray you have a lifetime of purpose and productivity.

Chapter Eighteen

A Spark of Enthusiasm

"So the LORD sparked the enthusiasm of Zerubbabel son of Shealtiel, governor of Judah, and the enthusiasm of Jeshua son of Jehozadak, the high priest, and the enthusiasm of the whole remnant of God's people. They began to work on the house of their God, the LORD of Heaven's Armies."
Haggai 1:14 (NLT)

As I think about coming to the end of this book, I am asking the Lord, "Have I included everything You want? Lord, what is important for me on put on these pages?" And what you are about to read is the result of that prayer.

This important story is a strong message of encouragement and challenge. It's about priorities, obedience, and consequences. It explains why (at times) God might withhold a blessing and what we should do about it. It is found in the book of Haggai. I know … who studies Haggai? I hope you will be glad you did! You can find this little book of the Bible tucked away near the end of the Old Testament. Actually, go to Matthew and turn the pages left two chapters. Haggai is just two chapters long, and I hope you will take time to read the story.

Let me give you a little background and set the stage for what we will be learning. Haggai was a prophet, which means he was a messenger of the Lord. He ministered to God's people for four months (around

520 BC) and then disappeared from recorded biblical history. His message was stern and direct.

The Temple in Jerusalem had been destroyed. King Cyrus allowed the Jews to return to their homeland to rebuild their Temple (the Lord's house). They began the work, but it soon stopped. And the Lord had something to say about that through His messenger Haggai. The purpose of Haggai's message was to call the people to **return, rebuild, and complete** the assignment the Lord had given them. He called the people to action and to put God first. He challenged them to reorder their priorities according to God's will. It is extremely applicable to us today!

Read Haggai 1:1–14 (NLT):

On August 29 of the second year of King Darius's reign, the LORD gave a message through the prophet Haggai to Zerubbabel son of Shealtiel, governor of Judah, and to Jeshua son of Jehozadak, the high priest. "This is what the LORD of Heaven's Armies says: The people are saying, 'The time has not yet come to rebuild the house of the LORD.'" Then the LORD sent this message through the prophet Haggai: "Why are you living in luxurious houses while my house lies in ruins? This is what the LORD of Heaven's Armies says: Look at what's happening to you! You have planted much but harvest little. You eat but are not satisfied. You drink but are still thirsty. You put on clothes but cannot keep warm. Your wages disappear as though you were putting them in pockets filled with holes!

"This is what the LORD of Heaven's Armies says: Look at what's happening to you! Now go up into the hills, bring down timber, and rebuild my house. Then I will take pleasure in it and be honored, says the Lord. You hoped for rich harvests, but they were poor. And when you brought your harvest home, I blew it away. Why? Because my house lies in ruins, says the LORD of Heaven's Armies, while all of you are busy building your own fine houses. It's because of you that the heavens withhold the dew and the earth produces no crops. I have called for a drought on your fields and hills—a drought to wither the grain and grapes and olive trees and all your other crops, a drought to starve you and your livestock and to ruin everything you have worked so hard to get."

Then Zerubbabel son of Shealtiel, and Jeshua son of Jehozadak, the high priest, and the whole remnant of God's people began to obey the message from the LORD their God. When they heard the words of the prophet Haggai, whom the LORD their God had sent, the people feared the LORD. Then Haggai, the LORD's messenger, gave the people this message from the LORD: "I am with you, says the LORD!" So the LORD sparked the enthusiasm of Zerubbabel son of Shealtiel, governor of Judah, and the enthusiasm of Jeshua son of Jehozadak, the high priest, and the enthusiasm of the whole remnant of God's people. They began to work on the house of their God, the LORD of Heaven's Armies, on September 21 of the second year of King Darius's reign.

Oh, there is so much here I want us to unpack! Here's the short list of circumstances and conditions:

- The Temple in Jerusalem had been destroyed (which was a symbol of God's presence).
- The Lord gave His people an assignment through His prophet Haggai.
- They began the work.
- Opposition came and they stopped the work.
- Their priorities shifted.
- Their interest and enthusiasm faded.
- Their passion vanished.
- The people complained.
- Apathy set in.
- The work ended … for fifteen years!
- God's blessing was withheld.
- God sent a message that He was with them.
- They began to obey and do the work again.
- God sparked their enthusiasm!

PROBLEM: There arose a **conflict of interest**!

After they started doing what the Lord asked them to do, they didn't like doing it. So, they started doing something different. Instead of building the Lord's house, they started building their own houses.

They became self-focused and self-centered. They wanted to do what they wanted to do.

When this priority shift occurred, consequences occurred. What they failed to realize was that their **adversity** was a result of their **disobedience**.

SOLUTION: The Lord gave them instruction: **"Consider your ways"** (Hag. 1:7 KJV).

This means to think carefully about your action, lives, and your decisions. What are you doing?

They had gotten side-tracked and distracted with their own stuff and did not make the Lord's stuff a priority in their lives. They became more concerned with building their own homes than building God's house. God sent Haggai to get them back to God's assignment, God's work, and God's values. He challenged the people to **move forward** in the work of the Lord. He encouraged them about God's faithfulness and God's promises.

> **Think carefully about your action, lives, and your decisions.**

Haggai called them back to action. However, after fifteen years, the work was still not complete. I want to share one thing that bothered me about that this. The Lord pointed this out and got me thinking about it. They started building. Then they stopped building. Which means the stones, the building material, and all the rubble was just laying around everywhere.

So, they walked around and in and out of the rubble, the ruins, and the broken-down places for fifteen years. Apparently, it didn't bother them anymore. They grew accustomed to it being "just the way it is." I am not a fan of the phrase: "It is what it is!" Hey, it is what it is … but it was never intended to be that way!

They did what culture tells us to do: "Learn to live with your new normal." But the Lord was saying, "Don't leave it like this—fix it!"

Personal application: Does this sound like anything going on in your life? Have you been walking around broken places and shattered pieces of your life … for years, perhaps saying, "That's just the way things are. I didn't break it; someone else did. I didn't make this mess. I just have to live with it."

No, you don't!
The Lord isn't asking if you are the one who **BROKE** it.
He is asking if you will be the one to **REBUILD** it!

The people around them did not want the people of God to make progress on the work of God. They frustrated the plans and opposed the rebuilding project. This led to a period of great discouragement. The walls were not being repaired. The hopes of the people evaporated. Apathy set in because their assignment became hard. Then a famine hit the land. And the Lord had something to say about WHY the famine came:

> Look at what's happening to you! You have planted much but harvest little. You eat but are not satisfied. You drink but are still thirsty. You put on clothes but cannot keep warm. Your wages disappear as though you were putting them in pockets filled with holes! (Haggai 1:5–6 NLT)

When we ignore, neglect, or walk away from God's assignments, even our best efforts may feel empty and fruitless. They worked but saw little reward.

> "Seek the Kingdom of God above all else, and live righteously, and he will give you everything you need" (Matt. 6:33 NLT).

Focus Verse

"So the LORD sparked the enthusiasm of Zerubbabel son of Shealtiel, governor of Judah, and the enthusiasm of Jeshua son of Jehozadak, the high priest, and the enthusiasm of the whole remnant of God's people. They began to work on the house of their God" (Hag. 1:14 NLT).

Connecting the Dots

What lessons can we learn from this story and their experience with the Lord?

1. **The Lord gives us assignments.** When you stay attentive to the Lord, He gives you *clear vision, divine energy, renewed passion, fresh ideas, and creative solutions* to complete your God-given assignments and purpose, which makes life meaningful and successful.

2. **Consider your ways**. Keep the main thing the main thing. It's been said that good is the enemy of the best. Good things can get shifted into first place while the best thing gets sidelined.

3. **Climb the hill and get the wood!** The Lord tells His people in Haggai 1:8 (NLT) what will bring Him pleasure, what will honor Him, and what He wants them to do: "Now go up into the hills, bring down timber, and rebuild my house. Then I will take pleasure in it and be honored, says the LORD." I find it interesting that He didn't say, "Cross the street and get the wood," or "Go down to the valley and get the wood." They had to climb the hill—not an easy task. I may be reading too much into this, but it feels like He wants us to come up higher even when the climb is difficult. And I know what some of you may be thinking: *Debbie, you don't know what I have been through lately. I am hurt. I am exhausted. I am overwhelmed. I am _____* (you fill in the blank). You may say things like:

"My knee has been hurting." Well, get a brace, climb the hill, and get the wood.

"I've been in tears over loss." Well, get some tissues, climb the hill, and get the wood.

"I'm all alone." Well, get a friend, climb the hill, and get the wood.

You get the message: CLIMB THE HILL, GET THE WOOD, AND REBUILD THE LORD'S HOUSE.

4. **Finish the work of the Lord—WITH ENTHUSIASM!**
   God wanted them to be involved in His work and building His house.

To be quite transparent, the fast pace and unexpected circumstances as of late have left me somewhat disillusioned. With things happening in my family, burying people I love, and transitions at work and in our church, changes are happening fast, and hard things continue to present themselves. No doubt you relate in some way—the stock market has tanked, gas prices have skyrocketed, and the list goes on! I don't know … stuff happens!

When I pulled up to my desk to meet with the Lord, all I could say was, "I'm sorry! I am sorry I am not more excited and enthusiastic about ministry right now. I wish I were. I wish I were here with more excitement and momentum and energy, but the truth is … I'm just here." Be assured I gave Him all my reasons for why I felt this way. And ever so tenderly I heard Him say, "There is never a good reason to stop working on the Lord's house. Now, climb the hill, get the wood, and rebuild the Lord's house."

See, I am very much like God's people at this time. I had let things in my world crowd out the things of God. The Bible says He gives us the Holy Spirit to work in and through us to accomplish His work. "For God is working in you, giving you the desire and the power to do what pleases him" (Phil. 2:13 NLT).

Side note: I actually have a reminder set on my phone for 2:13 every day to remind me that I have been given not only the desire, but also the power to do what pleases the Lord. Not to mention the enthusiasm! I didn't know the Lord sparked enthusiasm! I have now made that a regular part of my prayers. Haggai encouraged the people as they worked. He assured them of God's presence, God's power, and God's divine enthusiasm! In Haggai 2:9 (NLT), the Lord said, "The future glory of this Temple will be greater than its past glory, says the LORD of Heaven's Armies. And in this place I will bring peace. I, the LORD of Heaven's Armies, have spoken!"

Make It Personal

Have you been making excuses for finishing the work God has called you to do?

_____

_____

Do you have unfinished business with the Lord?

_____

_____

Do you need to rearrange your schedule, reclaim God's promises, and rebuild God's house?

_____

_____

Haggai challenged God's people to respond enthusiastically to God's work. I'd like to do the same.

Lord, would You please spark the enthusiasm of your people!

Chapter Nineteen

Hinge-Point Moments

"And they shall comfort you, when ye see their ways and their doings: and ye shall know that I have not done without cause all that I have done in it, saith the Lord GOD."
Ezekiel 14:23 (KJV)

Events and experiences create opportunities. And people use opportunities in different ways. History records great stories of men and women who seized an opportunity and stepped out in tremendous courage amidst great danger, uncertainty, and extreme risk. These people were from all walks of life, ages, races, and socioeconomic backgrounds. The one thing they had in common is that they were presented with a hinge-point moment in life.

I am thinking of people like Billy Graham, Martin Luther King Jr., Rosa Parks, Corrie Ten Boom, Mother Teresa, and Charlie Kirk. At the least, they started a worldwide movement, and at best—they changed the world.

Biblical history and God's Word also record such people. I became familiar with them when the Lord developed this message through a recent time of uncertainty, confusion, and—to be completely transparent—a season of fear in my life.

After several weeks of intense time with the Lord, I found myself begging the Lord for direction, guidance, intervention, and probably more than anything, some relief! It was specifically regarding two major areas of my life.

The first was with my sweetheart, John Mark. We've been married forty-one years as I write this. As explained in a previous chapter, John Mark had a heart transplant on January 28, 2020. (Oh, that was a fun year—said no one ever!) We walked through an urgent battle for his life for several months while he was in ICU awaiting a heart.

Fast forward to heart transplant recovery, which has taken years. He was unable to fully recover due to nerve damage in his chest and right arm, including fingers. At a doctor's appointment (during my season of confusion and fear), we were told: "**If it weren't for** nerve damage, you would be almost 100 percent recovered."

That phrase—"If it weren't for"—just added to my confusion and, to be completely honest, my frustration. If it weren't for THIS … then why do we have THIS?!

Our family has told this funny story for years. It's a story about something that happened when John Mark was a little boy. He had a very tough cousin—a girl who was his age. One afternoon she was trying to fight him. But he couldn't win. John Mark told his mother, "If it weren't for her hitting me, I would beat her up!" When Jarrad got his first paycheck, he said, "If it weren't for taxes, I'd have a decent paycheck!" And if it weren't for chocolate chip cookies at Chick-fil-A, I would be a size six!

See, if you are in the generation that can finish this sentence: "If it weren't for bad luck …" you guessed it, "I'd have no luck at all." (If you could not finish it, the quote is from a seventies show called "Hee Haw," which I cannot even explain to you!)

Seriously, though, give it some thought: How would you finish the sentence, "If it weren't for …"?

The second area of our life that seemed out of control (and driving me crazy) was Jarrad's parole process. This was happening simultaneously with John Mark's heart transplant process. And although we had followed every single rule and jumped through all the hoops (many times over!), there was still extreme opposition to his parole. We were told if it weren't for the new warden, he would be released. Then he was told if it weren't for COVID-19, he would be released.

I felt like I was living at the mercy of "If it weren't for …" and I couldn't do one thing about it. UNTIL the Lord spoke about it. It might be hard for you to understand how this happened, but this is EXACTLY how it happened. The Lord dropped two words into my mind and into my heart. I knew it was from the Lord because I had never even said those two words in my life. I may have only heard them a time or two.

The two words seemed loud, and they were clear: *HINGE POINT*.

I'm sorry, what? And the words came again: *HINGE POINT*. "What is *hinge point*?" I said out loud. The Lord said to me, "This is a hinge-point moment in your life!" I had an idea of what a hinge was. And I knew what a defining moment in life was, but I had never thought of these two words together. So, I set out for a better understanding and a deeper meaning, knowing this had some sort of spiritual emphasis at this point of my life. Learning the meaning of *hinge* started this impactful journey for me. The word indicates flexibility for a turning point based on later circumstances, events, opinions, or decisions.

> **Flexibility for a turning point based on later circumstances, events, opinions, or decisions.**

So, get a picture of a hinge in your mind. Think of a hinge on a door. The hinge allows the door to swing one way and/or the other. The hinge also allows it to open to another place.

I knew immediately what the Lord was saying and showing me. These two major experiences were hinge-point moments in my life. And my willingness to be flexible and pivot to the purpose of God was hanging in the balance. I believe these two events were turning points or defining moments. Perhaps even experiences that could change the course of history.

Hinge-point moments serve as spiritual crossroads where God invites a person to pivot toward deeper trust, obedience, healing, or purpose. Like a hinge on a door, these moments open up a new space or direction in life, often swinging open the door of hope, redemption, and calling.

Psalm 73:16–17 (CSB) says, "When I tried to understand this, it seemed hopeless until I entered God's sanctuary. Then I understood their destiny."

It goes on to say in verses 21–22: "When I became embittered and my innermost being was wounded, I was stupid and didn't understand; I was an unthinking animal toward you." At times in our spiritual journey, we are not going to understand on this side of heaven why things are playing out the way they are. Therefore, recognizing hinge-point moments is extremely important. These are times when the enemy of our soul seeks to embitter our innermost being and we can get hung up on "if it weren't for" situations instead of becoming a hinge on which the will of God can turn.

Application questions: Are you being flexible to all the Lord is allowing in your life? Are you pivoting to the purposes of God?

Your problem is not your problem; your perspective of your problem is the problem. I know what some of you might be thinking: *Debbie, I am so close to the edge right now that if I make one small pivot in the wrong direction, I'm going over. I am almost over the edge already and I don't see any room to pivot.*

HARD PLACES are often **HINGE-POINT** moments. **Pivotal places** are used to serve the **purposes of God**.

Psalm 40:1–3 says:

> *I waited patiently for the LORD; he turned to me and heard my cry. He lifted me out of the slimy pit, out of the mud and mire; he set my feet on*

a rock **[THIS IS A PIVOT!]** *and* **gave me a firm place to stand**. *He put a new song in my mouth, a hymn of praise to our God. Many will see and fear the* LORD *and put their trust in him. (emphasis and insert mine)*

In working through hinge-point moments with the Lord, I'm like, "Yeah, I'm gonna need to see this in Scripture, please." And I was shocked at the number of hinge-point moments I found and people who experienced turning points where their faith was deepened, God was glorified, and the world was changed just a little bit.

Hinge-Point Moments (Biblical Examples):

1. **Mary** said, "I am the servant of the Lord; let it be to me according to your word" (Luke 1:38 ESV).
2. **Joshua** said, "But as for me and my house, we will serve the LORD" (Josh. 24:15 ESV).
3. **Shadrach, Meshach, and Abednego** said, "The God whom we serve is able to save us. He will rescue us from your power, Your Majesty. But even if he doesn't, we want to make it clear to you, Your Majesty, that we will never serve your gods or worship the gold statue you have set up" (Dan. 3:17–18 NLT).

Now, let me show an occasion when someone did NOT pivot to the purposes of God.

4. **The Israelites** said things like: "We cannot do this. It is impossible. We do not believe God" (see Numbers 13).
5. **Saul** acted according to his own reasoning, tried to justify disobedience, and prioritized appearance and social status over God's commands. He regularly blamed others and harbored hatred in his heart.

And lastly …

6. **Benaiah** said—actually, the Bible does not record anything he said. But the Bible does record this about him: "He did many heroic deeds, which included killing two champions of

Moab. Another time, on a snowy day, he chased a lion down into a pit and killed it" (2 Sam. 23:20 NLT).

My paraphrase: His life screamed, "With God's help, I will defeat the lions (the enemies) in my life!" We have to take a closer look into this guy! Benaiah came to a hinge point-moment in his life. But the thing is he never said a word. No statement of Benaiah was ever recorded in Scripture. But his actions—his behavior—made a huge statement!

Focus Verse

"And they shall comfort you, when ye see their ways and their doings: and ye shall know that I have not done without cause all that I have done in it, saith the Lord God"
(Ezek. 14:23 KJV).

Connecting the Dots

There is a book inspired by this man called *In a Pit with a Lion on a Snowy Day* by Mark Batterson. Benaiah is one of the most obscure yet courageous people in the Bible. His hinge-point moment, recorded in Scripture, was a blessed and audacious act that left no regrets.

Second Samuel 23:20–21 (MSG) says:

> *Benaiah son of Jehoiada from Kabzeel was a vigorous man who accomplished a great deal. He once killed two lion cubs in Moab. Another time, on a snowy day, he climbed down into a pit and killed a lion. Another time he killed a formidable Egyptian. The Egyptian was armed with a spear and Benaiah went against him with nothing but a walking stick; he seized the spear from his grip and killed him with his own spear.*

This story begs the question: Who chases lions? AND on a snowy day at that? I can hardly walk to my car on a snowy day without falling!

Please try to imagine it—picture It! It was snowy, slippery, wet, and no doubt a hard-to-run-in-the-snow kind of day. I don't want to take too much liberty with Scripture, but the facts are:

- He chased down a lion.
- He jumped into the pit WITH the lion.
- He killed the lion.
- All of this happened on a snowy day!

I just wonder … did he shake off the snow and say, "I'll never hear you roar at me again!" He could have said, "If it weren't for that lion, I would not be so full of fear."

Note to self: Stop running from what you are afraid of!

We have a choice! *Hinge* to the positive side! Here's a positive twist on "If it weren't for …"

If it weren't for the cross, we would never have victory over anything.

> *"Lead me by your truth and teach me, for you are the God who saves me. All day long I put my hope in you" (Ps. 25:5 NLT).*

Your greatest regret at the end of your life may be the lions you didn't chase. Let's not look back longingly on risks not taken, opportunities not seized, and dreams not pursued.

Stop running away from what scares you most and start chasing the God-ordained opportunities that cross your path.

I think Benaniah made a hinge-point statement: "With God's help, I will defeat the lions in my life!" Benaiah's name means "Jehovah has built."

For some of us, the enemy has been roaring at us for years! There's probably something specific he keeps roaring about too! For years, he has roared at me about the two things I mentioned at the beginning of this story: my husband and my son. And it scared me. The evidence he was roaring about was real. Sometimes I could not hear what the Lord was saying about them because what the enemy was saying was so loud.

Who chases lions? YOU DO!

Hinge-Point People

Please allow me to give you a few more people that you can look up on your own (since you have Twenty Minutes a Day for the Rest of Your Life).

Record their hinge-point moments and the statement or actions they made:

1. Rahab
2. Deborah
3. Hosea
4. Paul
5. Sampson
6. Jael
7. Daniel (I bet he and Benaiah had some great talks about lions!)
8. Habakkuk
9. Esther
10. David

Oh, I have to just say this one thing about Daivd. We all know David to be "a man after God's own heart." That phrase comes from Acts 13:22. But the verse does not end there; there is actually a semi- colon and then the Bible tells us WHY he was considered to be a man after God's own heart: "God testified concerning him: 'I have found David son of Jesse, a man after my own heart; he will do everything I want him to do'" (Acts 13:22).

Well, well. Do tell. I hope you see the connection (the hinge if you will). The REASON God called him that was BECAUSE he did everything God wanted him to do.

Make It Personal

How are you doing with everything God has asked you to do?

You might be at a hinge-point moment in your life. Your future might depend on your next pivot.

It's not so much what happened—it's what happens next that is so important!

History has thrust a challenge upon us corporately. The Lord has thrust a challenge upon us personally.

Maybe the thing you hate right now, the thing you are wondering, "WHY is this happening? WHY is God doing this?" Girl, He is setting you up to pivot and that will lead to a hinge-point place in your life. He is positioning you for a pivot and that pivot has a purpose.

You know by now if you have read through this book that I am a weirdo. I admit it. I think in weird ways, I do weird things, and I ask weird questions. So, I asked the Lord, "Can a person set up their own hinge-point moment with You?"

The answer I heard back was YES!

Don't forfeit your hinge-point moments!

When David picked up five stones, he created a hinge-point moment. When Jonah decided to take the wrong boat, he created a hinge-point moment. When the woman with the issue of blood touched the helm of Jesus's garment, she created a hinge-point moment.

Develop a hinge-point statement. Create your own hinge-point moment.

Challenge: Don't underperform your pivotal places and don't forfeit your hinge-point moments!

"March on with courage, my soul!" (Judg. 5:21 NLT).

Prayer: *Awaken us to Your Word and Your ways and arm us with strength for the battle!*

Chapter Twenty

Guidance, Grit, and Growth

> *"The LORD will guide you continually,*
> *giving you water when you are dry*
> *and restoring your strength.*
> *You will be like a well-watered garden,*
> *like an ever-flowing spring."*
> Isaiah 58:11 (NLT)

The last chapter.

Although this is the end of many words, I pray those words have spoken life to you! I pray this book is a blessing to the Lord and a benefit to you. His instruction was clear from the beginning: "This is what the LORD, the God of Israel, says: Write down for the record everything I have said to you" (Jer. 30:2 NLT). Let the record of my life declare that I have found the Lord faithful! Through tragedy, unexpected difficulty, painful circumstances, things I hated, and things I loved—He. Is. Faithful!

> *"For the word of the LORD is right, and all His work is done in faithfulness"* (Ps. 33:4 NASB).

Every revelation from the Lord comes with an invitation to adjust our lives to it. I'd like to leave you with a few "best practices" for spiritual growth.

"So pay attention to how you hear. To those who listen to my teaching, more understanding will be given. But for those who are not listening, even what they think they understand will be taken away from them" (Luke 8:18 NLT).

Ten Tips to Fast-Track Your Spiritual Growth

I adapted these steps from Psalm 119:9–16 (NLT):

1. OBEYING Your Word (v. 9)
2. FOLLOWING Your ways (vv. 9–10)
3. HIDING Your Word (v. 11)
4. TALKING Your Word (v. 13)
5. DELIGHTING in Your Word (v. 14)
6. STUDYING Your Word (v. 15)
7. REFLECTING Your ways (v. 15)
8. DELIGHTING in Your principles (v. 16)
9. REMEMBERING Your Word (v. 16)
10. Twenty Minutes a Day for the Rest of Your Life! (You totally should have seen that one coming by now!)

> *"So take a new grip with your tired hands and strengthen your weak knees" (Heb. 12:12 NLT).*

And here is another "best practice" 12:12 verse that will be helpful to you!

> *"Be joyful in hope, patient in affliction, faithful in prayer" (Rom. 12:12).*

Charles Spurgeon once said in a sermon, "It is not possible for him to refuse to hear prayer which is based upon his promise and offered in faith."

When prayer is not our desire, we should strive to make it our discipline. When it is not your preference, we should make it your practice.

Years ago, I was in a leadership conference and Andy Stanley shared five things that are essential for deepening and expanding our faith and prayer life. These have become foundational elements of my life. As these things are put into practice and implemented into our lives, we will be anchored and grow strong in our relationship with the Lord (and others).

Five Things God Uses to Grow Your Faith (by Andy Stanley):
1. Practical biblical teaching
2. Private disciplines
3. Providential relationships
4. Pivotal circumstances
5. Personal ministry[19]

Pivotal circumstances are often defining moments in our lives. They can be some beloved event or circumstance, or they can be a time of crisis. There are many stories in God's Word where He used a crisis to cause someone to turn to God and get serious about their faith. We have talked through many of these throughout this book, and I encourage you to yield to the purpose of God in everything, especially painful things.

Pain has a way of twisting our thinking, hijacking our emotions, and crashing our decisions. The Lord often takes us to unexpected places for unknown reasons. And it is likely we won't understand it this side of heav-

> **When prayer is not our desire, we should strive to make it our discipline.**

en. But we can trust that He knows what the future is for us as we go through those hard things. He knows the lessons we can learn as we hang on to Him and His Word.

One hard lesson I had to learn in seasons of suffering, sorrow, or loss was to grieve the death of my hopes and dreams. God was working toward something I could not see and did not understand. But until I could let go of one, I could not receive the other. This writing below

---

19   Andy Stanley, *Five Things God Uses to Grow Your Faith Study Participant's Guide* (HarperChristian Resources, 2009).

was one of the best explanations of the process of letting go that I
have ever read. I hope it is helpful to you.

"Death of a Dream (A Prayer for the Disappointed)" by Douglas
Kaine McKelvey:

> Oh Christ, in whom the final fulfillment of all hope is held and
> secure,
> I bring to you now the weathered fragments of my former dreams,
> the rent patches of hopes worn thin,
> the shards of some shattered image of life as I once thought it
> would be.
> What I so wanted has not come to pass,
> I invested my hopes in desires that returned only sorrow and
> frustration.
> Those dreams, like glimmering faerie feasts, could not sustain me,
> and in my head I know that you are sovereign even over this—
> over my tears, my confusion, and my disappointment.
> But I still feel, in this moment,
> as if I have been abandoned,
> as if you do not care that these hopes
> have collapsed to rubble.
> And yet I know this is not so.
> You are the sovereign of my sorrow.
> You apprehended a wider sweep with wiser eyes than mine.
> My history hears the fingerprints of grace.
> You were always faithful,
> though I could not always trace quick evidence of your presence
> in my pain,
> yet did you remain at work, lurking in the wings,
> sifting all my splinterings for bright embers
> that might be breathed into more eternal dreams.
> I have seen so oft in retrospect,
> How you had not neglected me,
> but had, with a master's care,
> flared my desire like silver in a crucible to burn away some lesser
> longing,

and bring about your better vision.
So let me remain tender now,
to how you would teach me.
My disappointments reveal so much about my own agenda for
my life,
and the ways I quietly demand that it should play out:
free of conflict, free of pain, free of want.
My dreams are all so small.
Your bigger purpose has always been for my greatest good,
that I would day-to-day be fashioned into a more fit vessel
for the indwelling of your Spirit,
and molded into a more compassionate emissary of your coming
Kingdom.
And you, in love, will use all means to shape my heart into those
perfect forms.
So let this disappointment do its work.
My truest hopes have never failed,
they have merely been buried beneath the shoveled muck of
disillusion,
or encased in a carapace of self-serving desire.
It is only false hopes that are brittle,
shattering like shells of thin glass,
to reveal the diamond hardness of the unshakeable eternal hopes
within.
So shake and shatter all that hinder my growth, O God.
Unmask all false hopes,
that my one true hope might shine out unclouded and undimmed.
So let me be tutored by this new disappointment.
Let me listen to its holy whisper,
that I may release at last these lesser dreams.
That I might embrace the better dreams you dream for me,
and for your people, and for your kingdom, and for your creation.
Let me join myself to these,
investing all hope in the one hope that will never come undone
or betray those who place their trust in it.
Teach me to hope, O Lord,

always and only in you.
You are the King of my collapse.
You answer not what I demand,
but what I do not even know what to ask.
Now take this dream, this husk, this chaff of my desire,
and give it back reformed and remade
according to your better vision,
or do not give it back at all.
Here in the ruins of my wrecked expectation,
let me make this confession:
Not my dreams, O Lord, not my dreams,
but yours, be done. Amen.
(Romans 8:28; Ephesians 2:10)[20]

God often begins bringing His will about in a way that looks like a mistake. I have now built up enough history with Him that I know to watch, wait, and not confuse His *ways* with His *will*. I'm learning not to confuse *what* He is doing with *how* He is doing it.

> **God communicates with us through His Word, so read it daily to stay connected to Him.**

Example: When we were praying for Jarrad's deliverance from addiction, I was so confused why God would allow such circumstances. It did not seem like, nor look like, nor feel like deliverance to me.

Biblical example: Joseph. What was God's will for Joseph? His will was for him to be ruler over the land of Egypt. God told Joseph this in a dream. Next, we see Joseph in a pit begging for his life, betrayed by his brothers, sold into slavery, and then thrown into prison having been falsely accused of a crime. He sat there for years, and it certainly didn't appear that God was bringing about His will. It appeared and felt like a waste of time. And he likely felt forgotten by God. When, actually, God was working

---

20   Douglas Kaine McKelvey, *Every Moment Holy, Volume I: New Liturgies for Daily Life* (The Rabbit Room, 2017).

out His will for Joseph through every painful event He allowed to happen to him.

God communicates with us through His Word, so read it daily to stay connected to Him. God communicates through His Son, Jesus Christ, so talk to Him often during your day. God communicates through His Holy Spirit, so pay attention to the way He speaks to your heart. I've also found that God communicates to me through creation, so spend time in what He has created.

> *"Come close to God, and God will come close to you" (Jas. 4:8 NLT).*

> *"The LORD is close to all who call on him, yes, to all who call on him in truth. He grants the desires of those who fear him; he hears their cries for help and rescue them" (Ps. 145:18–19 NLT).*

> *"All Scripture is breathed out by God and profitable for teaching, for reproof, for correction, and for training in righteousness, that the man of God may be complete, equipped for every good work" (2 Tim. 3:16–17 ESV).*

> *"All Scripture is inspired by God and is useful to teach us what is true and to make us realize what is wrong in our lives. It corrects us when we are wrong and teaches us to do what is right. God uses it to prepare and equip his people to do every good work" (2 Tim. 3:16–17 NLT).*

In 2 Timothy, Paul encourages Timothy and us to do these things:

1. Stay strong.
2. Fan the flames.
3. Be bold.
4. Develop confident endurance.
5. Fight opposition.
6. Stay grounded in God's Word.
7. Be steadfast in your faith.
8. Endure hardship like a soldier.
9. Be diligent in your devotion to Jesus.
10. Utilize the gifts God has given you.

I feel led to close this book with a story of a personal challenge the Lord spoke to me. I hope it is encouraging and challenging to you as well.

When John Mark was in ICU awaiting a heart transplant, I got to know the families of the other patients awaiting transplants. The lady across the hall from us was awaiting a heart and lung transplant. One afternoon about three p.m., alerts began to sound in her room. Alarms were going off and doctors and nurses came running down the hallway and immediately you could hear the flurry of activity in her room. I stepped to the edge of our room, and I could hear the urgency of the activity occurring. I did not see any of it, but I heard every minute of it. Doctors and nurses were scrambling. There was an obvious emergency. Doctors and nurses were scrambling to take care of her. Someone shouted, "She's unresponsive! She's unresponsive!" And someone else began to shout orders of things to do. They shocked her heart, what seemed like many times, with the defibrillator. They intensely worked on her for thirty to forty minutes. But she did not survive.

One by one, I watched them walk out of her room. They came out with a look of despair on their faces. They tried so hard to get her body to respond to intervention that would save her life. But she did not respond. As I stood in the hallway with tears rolling down my face, this is what the Lord said in my spirit, "Debbie Stuart, do not be unresponsive to Me!"

They were trying to do everything they could to help her, to heal her, and to cause her to live. But she did not respond to those things. I do not want to be unresponsive to the things of God, even when those things cause me pain. I do not want to be passive, neglectful, or inattentive to all God is doing in my life. We are the Lord's servants; let it be as He desires (from Luke 1:38). Make the rest of your life the best of your life!

Focus Verse

"The LORD will guide you continually, giving you water when you are dry and restoring your strength. You will be like a well-watered garden, like an ever-flowing spring"
(Isa. 58:11 NLT).

Connecting the Dots

We have a promise from our focus verse that the Lord will guide us—not just for a day or a week—but continually. He refreshes us when we are thirsty for His Word, and our strength is restored as we respond to the leading of God by His Spirit. I want to be like that spring that never stops flowing and the garden that flourishes because it is well watered and taken care of. That's what God does. He feeds, nourishes, and takes care of us in a way that enables us to respond to His will.

Make It Personal

As we conclude this book, I pray that you have seen how God works through every hardship, loss, and crisis to complete that which He has begun in us. Our final assignment is not a command, but a choice.

Fasting has been effective in my life, so I want to offer information and resources for fasting and prayer on the following pages. Who knows—perhaps this is what you have been waiting for to apply to your prayer life. May it be a blessing to you.

FASTING

Purpose of Fasting:

- **Giving up something you love for something you love more!**
- Draw closer to the Lord (see Joel 2:12–15). The Lord is not moved by fasting itself.

Reasons to Fast (Reasons vary. Purpose does not!):

- When facing *major decisions*
- In preparation for a *great work* or major event(s)
- When we are in *trouble*
- At the beginning of a *new year*
- When in *repentance*
- When we need *specific and clear direction* about something or someone
- When someone else is in *trouble* but not *spiritually mature* enough to fast for themselves (i.e., a child)
- When our *health* is attacked or *seriously threatened*
- When the Lord *leads/calls* us to fast
- When facing a *financial need* (This was the case with Ezra's fast and the leaders returning from captivity back to Jerusalem carrying the temple treasury with them. There would be thieves along the way so they fasted for God's protection.)
- Personal examples: I fast on the seventeenth of each month (for my son whose baseball number is 17), on the first Monday of each month for ministry needs, and on the first Friday of each month for family needs, etc.

Types of Fasts:

- **Full/Complete Fast:** One would drink only liquids—especially water. One may consider taking in other liquids such as 100 percent fruit or vegetable juices or a clear broth (vegetable, chicken, or beef). Through prayer, determine the number of days to set for your full fast. Check with your doctor first.
- **Partial Fast:** One would limit certain foods for a prolonged time period (i.e., meats), or abstain entirely from all foods for a portion of the day(i.e., until three p.m.).
- **Daniel Fast**: Inspired by Daniel 10. One would fast from all meats, breads, sweets, and any drink except water for a specific set period of time (Daniel's fast in the Bible lasted twenty-one days). Actually, one would eat only fruits and vegetables (no rice—rice is not a vegetable, but a grain) and drink

water. Always check with your doctor especially if you have medical conditions.

- Some people choose to fast from **all media**: no TV, radio, phone, computer, newspaper, magazines, etc. This might be practical for a diabetic desiring to fast. It can also be effective when one is "addicted" to these things. Starve your flesh! Not only are you not giving yourself what you want, but you are giving yourself what you truly need. How might your life change if you substituted Bible study and prayer for the latest and greatest *whatever*?
- **True fasting** is from *food*. Keep that in mind when deciding.
- **Corporate Fasting:** This is between groups of believers for a specific purpose and yields powerful results. True, it involves others but still remains *private and personal*. Esther called a corporate fast among her people for protection against extreme danger (see Esther 4:16), and Samuel called for a corporate fast for national revival.

How Long Do I Fast?

Beginner: Start slowly. Do not start with a forty-day fast if you have never fasted before!

- One meal (for several days)
- One food/food group for a set amount of days/weeks
- Ask the Lord what HE wants YOU to do.

YOU DECIDE! IT'S BETWEEN YOU AND THE LORD!

Helpful Guidelines:

- Consider finding and enlisting a prayer partner or two!
- Keep a journal. Journaling helps pass the time and it helps keep you on task and focused on the Lord, not food. Record what you are hearing from the Lord and the new insights gained while fasting. Write down at the beginning of the fast your goals and intended gains from the fast. Decide the length of your fast and write down your dates in the form of a contract (**Beginning Date_____ End Date___).** Write

down the things you are fasting for. Record the results of your fast. Record your feelings—physically, emotionally, spiritually, mentally—during your fast.

- Fasting is *before the Lord*, not unto man.
- Let immediate family and close friends know what you are doing and check with your doctor (especially if you are diabetic).
- Rewards of fasting do not always come during the fast but after a time of fasting.
- Do not be legalistic when fasting. Be obedient, but not legalistic. Listen to the Lord.
- Do not police others whom you know are fasting themselves. Mind your own fast.
- Listen for the Lord about your fasting while you are fasting. He may speak to you about modifying your fast. Obey Him.
- Expect spiritual opposition during and perhaps even after your fast.

Principles of Fasting:

- When we renounce the natural, we release the supernatural.
- Fasting is a biblical discipline.
- Fasting is not just skipping a meal but rather replacing a meal in order to "feed" more fully on the Lord.
- Fasting may be physical discipline, but it is also a spiritual feat.
- Fasting breaks you out of the world's routine, humbles you, and brings you back to your first love, causing the roots of your relationship with Christ to grow deeper.
- Fasting invites Christ to share secrets with you about Himself, His plans, and His desires for you.
- Fasting is a powerful way to cleanse the body from toxins, over-nourishment. and disease. It brings with it renewed energy and good health.
- Fasting is a sacrifice born out of expectancy.
- Fasting causes you to be more sensitive to the things of the Holy Spirit. As your flesh dies, your spirit becomes more alive to Him, bringing you to a new level spiritually.
- Faith is required for fasting.

- The Holy Spirit is preparing you for what is ahead when He calls you to fast.
- Fasting enables us to discern between what we want and what we need.
- Fasting brings us in line with God's priorities.
- Life will seem to slow down when you are fasting.
- *Afflict* and *mourn* are words associated with fasting.
- Fasting itself is a constant prayer before God.
- Fasting breaks the yoke of bondage.

Recommended Reading/Resources:

- *Fasting* by Jentezen Franklin

Appendix

Inviting Jesus into your life is simple. Scripture tells us how:

> *Romans 3:23 (ESV) "For all have sinned and fall short of the glory of God. "*

> *Romans 10:9 (ESV) ""because, if you confess with your mouth that Jesus is Lord and believe in your heart that God raised him from the dead, you will be saved."*

> *Romans 10:13 (ESV) For "everyone who calls on the name of the Lord will be saved."*

Prayer:

Lord Jesus, I believe you sacrificed your life for my salvation and that God raised you from the dead that as I believe in you, I will have eternal life. I call upon your name in this moment confessing my sin and my need for a Savior. Please forgive me and teach me to live a life pleasing to you. Come into my life that I can have a personal relationship with you now and for all eternity. In Jesus Name, Amen.

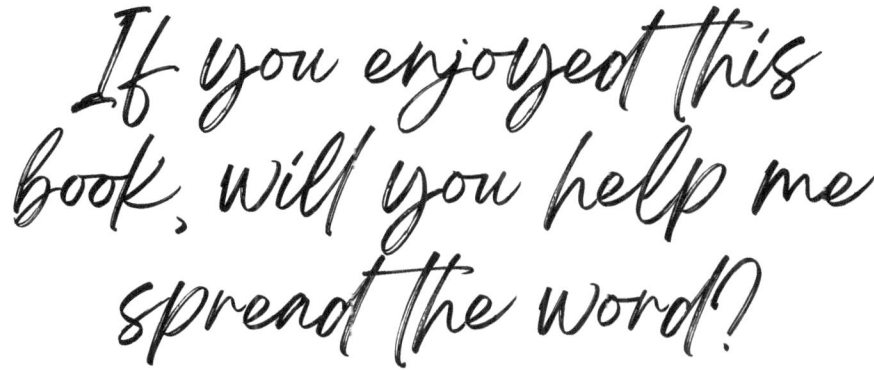

If you enjoyed this book, will you help me spread the word?

There are several ways you can help me get the word out about the message of this book ...

- Post a 5-Star review on Amazon.
- Write about the book on your Facebook, X, Instagram, LinkedIn—any social media you regularly use!
- If you blog, consider referencing the book, or publishing an excerpt from the book with a link back to my website. You have my permission to do this if you provide proper credit and backlinks.
- Recommend the book to friends—word-of-mouth is still the most effective form of advertising.

This is the third book in a series. You will find the first two by this author at Green Acres Baptist Church, 1607 Troup Hwy., Tyler, Texas. Phone: 903-525-1183. You may read messages from this author at www.greenacreswomen.org

Book One Title: ***20 Minutes a Day for the Rest of Your Life***

Book Two Title: ***20 Lessons Learned***

www.ingramcontent.com/pod-product-compliance
Lightning Source LLC
Chambersburg PA
CBHW051617120626
46551CB00014B/1827